BONUS
STEP-BY-STEP GUIDE
TO LEVERAGING
ChatGPT
IN YOUR DAILY WORK

FUTURE-READY
L&D PROFESSIONAL

UNLEASHING ADAPTABILITY AND GROWTH IN THE AGE OF RAPID CHANGE

"The only way to make sense out of change is to plunge into it,
move with it, and join the dance."
Alan Watts

FUTURE-READY
L&D PROFESSIONAL
UNLEASHING ADAPTABILITY AND GROWTH IN THE AGE OF RAPID CHANGE

"In a world of unprecedented change and complexity, the Future-Ready L&D Professional must be the torchbearer of adaptability, growth, and innovation. This book is your compass, guiding you through the uncharted territory of Learning and Development, empowering you to unlock the potential of your organization and its people to thrive in the age of rapid change."

Ross Thornley

Author of Moonshot Innovation, Decoding AQ, The Coach's Ultimate Guide to Leveraging Adaptability, The Leader's Ultimate Guide to Successful Transformation, and Future-Ready L&D Professional.

PREFACE

The world we live in today is one marked by an unprecedented rate of change, driven by rapid advancements in technology, globalization, and shifting workforce dynamics. In the midst of this transformation, learning and development (L&D) professionals play a vital role in ensuring that organizations are prepared and equipped to not only survive but thrive in the face of these challenges. The skills, knowledge, and capabilities that were once sufficient for success are no longer enough; we must now develop the adaptability and agility to continuously evolve, learn, and grow in response to the ever-changing landscape.

This book, "The Future-Ready L&D Professional: Unleashing Adaptability and Growth in the Age of Rapid Change," was born out of a desire to provide L&D professionals with the tools, insights, and strategies needed to effectively navigate this new world. The aim is to help L&D professionals become catalysts for change, empowering individuals and organizations to embrace adaptability and foster a culture of continuous growth and learning.

The journey begins with an exploration of the evolving role of L&D professionals in the 21st century, delving into the ways in which globalization, technological advancements, and the shift to remote and hybrid work environments have shaped the L&D landscape. This sets the stage for a comprehensive examination of the various aspects of designing future-ready learning programs, with a particular focus on identifying the key skills and competencies required for the future of work, and creating a culture of lifelong learning.

Next, the book addresses the unique challenges and opportunities presented by remote and hybrid work environments, offering practical guidance on how to adapt learning programs to these new contexts while maintaining engagement, collaboration, and accessibility. This is followed by an in-depth look at how L&D professionals can leverage technology to enhance their practice, including discussions on learning management systems, virtual and augmented reality, artificial intelligence, and learning analytics.

As we delve further into the realm of adaptive leadership, readers will gain valuable insights into the essence of adaptability and strategies for fostering innovation, creativity, and decision-making in uncertain times. This is complemented by practical advice on how to support the development of adaptive leaders, as well as measure the impact of adaptive leadership development initiatives.

The book concludes with an exploration of how to build a future-ready L&D community, offering tips on establishing partnerships, sharing knowledge and best practices, and embracing a growth mindset. Finally, a bonus chapter provides practical ways for L&D professionals to incorporate the capabilities of GPT-4, an AI-powered language model, into their daily work.

It is my sincere hope that this book will serve as a valuable resource for L&D professionals, enabling them to transform their practice and position themselves as future-ready leaders in an age of rapid change. May you find inspiration, knowledge, and practical tools within these pages that will empower you to unleash adaptability and growth in yourself, your organization, and the individuals you serve.

IN THE FACE OF RAPID CHANGE, ADAPTABILITY IS OUR GREATEST ALLY.

CONTENTS

CHAPTER 1: THE EVOLVING ROLE OF L&D PROFESSIONALS

1.1 THE CHANGING LANDSCAPE OF L&D

In today's fast-paced world, the role of learning and development (L&D) professionals has evolved significantly. Organizations are facing unprecedented levels of disruption, requiring them to adapt quickly and continuously to new technologies, market shifts, and global challenges. In this dynamic environment, L&D professionals are no longer just responsible for designing and delivering training programs; they have become strategic partners in driving organizational performance and resilience.

In this chapter, we will examine the key factors that have contributed to the changing landscape of L&D, including globalization, technology advancements, the shift towards remote work, and the increasing importance of agility and adaptability. We will also explore the implications of these changes for L&D professionals and the new skills and competencies they must develop to succeed in their evolving roles.

Traditional models of business success are no longer sufficient, as we stand at the forefront of a new era in business, adaptability has become a critical competency for organizations seeking to navigate uncertainty and capitalize on emerging opportunities.

1.2 GLOBALIZATION AND THE NEED FOR CONTINUOUS LEARNING

Globalization has transformed the way businesses operate, creating a more interconnected and interdependent world. As organizations expand their reach and compete in the global market, they encounter diverse cultures, languages, and business practices. This has led to a growing demand for employees who possess not only technical skills but also the ability to navigate the complexities of a global business environment. L&D professionals play a critical role in addressing these challenges by fostering a culture of continuous learning and adaptability within their organizations.

Technological advancements, shifting market demands, and evolving business models demand that employees remain agile and up-to-date with the latest knowledge and skills. This constant evolution also necessitates a shift in the traditional learning and development approach, moving away from one-time, event-based training programs to ongoing, personalized learning experiences that support employees throughout their careers.

Cultural awareness and cross-cultural communication have also become increasingly important in the globalized world.

Employees must be equipped with the skills to collaborate and communicate effectively with colleagues and clients from diverse backgrounds, understanding and respecting the nuances of different cultures. L&D professionals must prioritize the development of cultural competence, offering training programs that promote empathy, open-mindedness, and adaptability in the workforce.

Additionally, globalization has resulted in a more competitive job market, requiring organizations to invest in employee development to attract and retain top talent. By offering opportunities for continuous learning and professional growth, organizations demonstrate a commitment to their employees' success, leading to increased job satisfaction and loyalty.

So, based on the above overview, to address the demands of an increasingly globalized world, L&D professionals can:

→ **EMPHASIZE THE IMPORTANCE OF CONTINUOUS LEARNING:** ENCOURAGE A LEARNING MINDSET AND PROVIDE RESOURCES AND OPPORTUNITIES FOR EMPLOYEES TO UPDATE THEIR SKILLS AND KNOWLEDGE REGULARLY.

→ *SHIFT TOWARDS PERSONALIZED AND ONGOING LEARNING EXPERIENCES:* TRANSITION FROM TRADITIONAL TRAINING

METHODS TO MORE FLEXIBLE, PERSONALIZED LEARNING APPROACHES THAT SUPPORT EMPLOYEES THROUGHOUT THEIR CAREERS.

→ **DEVELOP CULTURAL COMPETENCE:** OFFER TRAINING PROGRAMS THAT FOSTER CULTURAL AWARENESS, EMPATHY, AND EFFECTIVE CROSS-CULTURAL COMMUNICATION SKILLS.

→ **INVEST IN EMPLOYEE COACHING & DEVELOPMENT:** ATTRACT AND RETAIN TOP TALENT BY DEMONSTRATING A COMMITMENT TO THE PERSONAL AND PROFESSIONAL GROWTH OF EMPLOYEES.

→ **INVEST IN ADAPTABILITY:** EQUIP EMPLOYEES WITH THE TOOLS AND MINDSET TO EMBRACE CHANGE AND THRIVE IN A RAPIDLY EVOLVING GLOBAL MARKET.

1.3 THE CORPORATE IMMUNE SYSTEM

Even if we—as an individual—are on-board with the concept of AQ and developing our adaptability muscles, we now face another challenge: how to make changes in such a way that the corporate immune-system response does not immediately reject and kill them! So before we even cover the new techniques and methodologies of fostering adaptability in your teams, we must address the corporate immune system–and the question of buy-in. This may not be a difficulty all organisations face—those working in SMEs may have smaller teams with greater alignment and agility. However, even small businesses will encounter major issues if they are attempting radical levels of change and find themselves forcing change upon people who aren't ready to embrace it!

The corporate immune system is a fairly well-known phenomenon at this point, but it is worth unpacking in more detail. Our immune system is designed to keep us safe from biological threats. However, sometimes, our body can be 'disrupted' by a virus or toxin, or we make a drastic change to our lifestyle or diet, and then the immune system has trouble identifying what is helpful and what is an enemy. This is an auto-immune disorder. It causes your defensive white blood cells to attack *everything* and dramatically weakens the body, sometimes even fatally. Hair falls out. Skin turns bloody and is covered in awful rashes. Energy levels plummet. The body is fighting a war with itself. This is a truly terrible thing to happen to anybody and it happens not just at a personal biological level, but also at a psychological and an organisational level.

But why? Why do people resist the very changes which might just save them?

Our AQ assessment measures individuals on a motivational continuum from playing-to-win to playing-to-protect. This might alternatively be considered as insight into whether someone is risk friendly or risk averse. People at the latter end of the continuum are more security-driven; they make calculated decisions based on risk assessment and protecting their assets. This isn't a "bad" thing, in any sense. Process and security-driven people can do well in roles that require meticulous precision or repetition or fastidious checking. We wouldn't want our accountant to take unnecessary risks with our finances, after all!

But as we prepare for technological displacement, many tasks we historically held dear will find themselves automated and replaced. Supporting the transition for those currently serving in these capacities will be a crucial challenge to overcome for virtually all businesses. Ensuring people feel connected, a sense of belonging and part of the collective, with a future contribution to serve, is a growing and important social aspect of every ethical business. We must commit to bringing all people with us into this new technology-driven world. However, someone who is more play-to-protect is unlikely to be a natural innovator, viewing change and innovation as a threat to security and well-being. Hence they can, almost literally, "attack".

Further to this, the ways in which an organization introduces innovation can often magnify the immune system problem. Innovation and R&D teams are commonly equipped to deliver value through efficiency and productivity. This is where the innovations of yesterday have borne reward, and further embedding behaviours aligned to these practices.

When it comes to cutting-edge innovation, to creating radical breakthrough ideas, organisations often recruit external consultants after trying and failing internally. Together with acquisition strategies to accelerate technological adoption and market advantage. This dynamically different culture, when added to the core, can experience significant friction, stress, and disconnect. Risking the loss of great people, talent and experience with it.

To drive and achieve radical transformation ("radical" is in relation to your own current state) can be antagonizing to the teams employed to maintain and grow "business-as-usual". To be honest, unless careful preparation and fertile ground exists within an organization, most will fail at this type of far-horizon value creation. The freedom, trust, space, tolerance for failure rates, and facilitation required is often vastly underestimated. Asking your teams and people, who have been responsible for mitigating risk, to now take not a little but a lot of risk, to dream and give birth to crazy ideas, is no simple behaviour switch and requires brain gymnastics even for the most creative in your teams.

Either way, the organization's immune system will often

attack any and all initiatives that don't look like previous successes.

SO WHAT IS THE SOLUTION?

To help neutralise a corporate immune system attack, organizations previously fostered a culture of highly adaptable and experimental employees separate from the core, attempting to give them freedom, time, and space to experiment, removing the governance and reporting lines for approvals and allowing autonomous execution. This encouraged the transformation process, which, alongside outside collaboration, helped develop the company's future lifeline. Now the most successful organizations are investing in highly adaptable leaders and workforces across the organization, not just at the edges and fringes, in a sand pit of their own. It must become a core competency for everyone within the organisation, to enable high levels of adaptability across the full spectrum, across the entire employee life-cycle, tenure, and hierarchy.

Simultaneously, bringing in measurement tools, platforms, and specialist coaches to psychologically and practically support your employees' transition with adaptability can be an effective way to reduce the negative immune system response. Transforming an organisation is not just about the organisation itself, but also about updating the mindsets and knowledge-base of the people who work for it so they are not "left behind" by organisational and industrial change. Together we must transform our organisation's antibodies (its white cells) into highly adaptable champions: red blood cells dedicated to driving innovation, and successfully navigating the wild waves of constant flux and change.

Changing the way people think, and the way you think, is not easy. It can be painful and sometimes torturous process that requires grit and determination. Figuring it out takes a level of bravery and, I would argue, a sense of adventure. Shifting our thinking shifts our reality. The same event or process that makes somebody very stressed, very awkward, very uncomfortable, can be joyful for someone else with the right mindset. It's a decision. It's not the path you take but the mindset with which you take the path. You could set out on a big adventure and it could be all about survival. Someone else could undertake the same adventure and it could be all about the experience and joy.

And so I urge you in whatever adventure you undertake, whatever transformation you aim for, to know that the adventure is not the reason why it's stressful and hard or why you are encountering huge seemingly un-scalable obstacles. It is your perspective and mindset that create them. If you, as an L&D Professional looking to intigate transformation, do it with optimism, do it with joy, do it with excitement and effervescence, that becomes infectious. It is important to make sure you're infecting your surroundings, your employees, your work-space, your colleagues, your friends—infecting them with energy, belief, vitality, and excitement.

Whilst I remain determined to create positive change in this world, I also recognise that there is no point achieving that change at the cost of all else. It's pointless to succeed in reaching a moonshot or a transformational goal, only to come out the other end near dead with exhaustion, stress, and a feeling of ill-will amongst the people you've been working with. To lose all of your emotional and physical resources and to kill the spirit of the team to get to the end is unhealthy and pretty unethical.

You want to arrive at each chapter of development with your energy and vitality still intact. Not only is this the best outcome for everyone, it's actually the best way to achieve the moonshot or transformation in the first place. When everyone is motivated, energised, and passionate, with purpose clearly aligned, you will harness the creative potential of those around. We can benefit from the 'red blood cell' effect of organisational champions.

1.4 TECHNOLOGY ADVANCEMENTS AND THE SHIFT TO DIGITAL LEARNING

The digital revolution has had a profound impact on the world of learning and development, with technology playing an increasingly significant role in shaping the way people acquire knowledge and skills. L&D professionals must stay abreast of these technological advancements and incorporate them into their strategies to create engaging, effective, and accessible learning experiences. The shift to digital learning has led to the emergence of new methods and tools, which are transforming traditional approaches to training and development.

E-Learning and Mobile Learning: The widespread adoption of the internet and mobile devices has made online learning accessible to a broader audience. E-learning and mobile learning platforms allow learners to access training materials anytime, anywhere, and at their own pace. L&D professionals must create engaging and interactive digital content that is responsive and accessible across various devices, ensuring an optimal learning experience for all users.

Learning Management Systems (LMS): An LMS is a centralized platform that enables organizations to manage, track, and deliver training programs. It streamlines the administration of learning initiatives, facilitates collaboration and communication among learners, and provides valuable data and insights into learner performance. L&D professionals should select an LMS that aligns with their organization's needs and goals, while offering features such as content creation, progress tracking, and reporting capabilities.

Blended Learning: This approach combines traditional face-to-face instruction with digital learning elements, providing a more holistic learning experience. By leveraging the strengths of both methods, L&D professionals can create more engaging and effective training programs. For example, Masterclass offers online courses taught by industry experts, which can be supplemented with in-person workshops or group discussions to deepen the learning experience.

MOOCs (Massive Open Online Courses) and Online Education Platforms: MOOCs and online education platforms, such as Outlier.org, democratize access to high-quality education by offering affordable, flexible, and scalable learning experiences. L&D professionals can use these platforms to provide employees with opportunities to gain new skills or deepen their knowledge in specific areas, enhancing their professional development.

Virtual Reality (VR) and Augmented Reality (AR) Training: VR and AR technologies offer immersive and interactive learning experiences by simulating real-world environments and scenarios. TaleSpin, for example, uses VR to create realistic training simulations for soft skills development, such as leadership, communication, and empathy. L&D professionals can incorporate VR and AR technologies to create engaging and practical training programs that lead to better retention and application of learned skills.

Adaptive Learning: This approach leverages advanced algorithms and data analytics to create personalized learning paths for individual learners, based on their strengths, weaknesses, and learning preferences. By tailoring the learning experience to each employee, L&D professionals can improve engagement, increase knowledge retention, and accelerate skill development.

Social Learning and Collaboration Tools: Social learning platforms and collaboration tools, such as Slack or Microsoft Teams, facilitate peer-to-peer learning and knowledge-sharing. By encouraging employees to engage in informal learning and collaborate with their colleagues, L&D professionals can foster a culture of continuous learning and development.

Gamification: Incorporating game elements, such as points, badges, and leaderboards, into the learning experience can increase engagement, motivation, and retention. L&D professionals can use gamification techniques to make learning more enjoyable and encourage friendly competition among employees.

By staying current with technology advancements and embracing digital learning tools and approaches, L&D professionals can create more effective, engaging, and accessible training programs that cater to the needs of modern learners. This will ultimately lead to a more skilled and adaptable workforce, ready to face the challenges of an ever-changing global market.

1.5 REMOTE WORK AND THE DEMAND FOR VIRTUAL LEARNING

The rise of remote work has created new challenges and opportunities for L&D professionals in delivering effective learning experiences to a geographically dispersed workforce. The demand for virtual learning solutions has surged, necessitating the adaptation of traditional training methods to suit remote and hybrid work environments. L&D professionals must address the unique aspects of remote work while leveraging technology to ensure that learning remains engaging, accessible, and impactful.

Accessibility and Flexibility: Remote employees require learning solutions that can be accessed from anywhere and at any time, allowing them to balance work and learning commitments. L&D professionals should prioritize the development of on-demand and self-paced learning experiences, such as e-learning modules or recorded webinars, that cater to the diverse needs and schedules of remote workers.

Communication and Collaboration: Building connections and fostering collaboration among remote employees can be challenging. L&D professionals should leverage digital communication and collaboration tools, such as video conferencing platforms, online forums, and chat applications, to facilitate real-time interaction and knowledge sharing among learners. These tools can be used to conduct virtual workshops, live Q&A sessions, or team-based learning activities, fostering a sense of community and shared learning experience.

Engagement and Interactivity: Virtual learning can sometimes lead to feelings of isolation and disengagement among remote employees. To counteract this, L&D professionals should design interactive learning experiences that encourage active participation and engagement. Techniques such as gamification, virtual breakout rooms, and real-time feedback can help maintain learners' interest and motivation throughout the learning process.

Technical Support and Infrastructure: To ensure seamless virtual learning experiences, L&D professionals must invest in the necessary technical infrastructure and support systems. This includes selecting appropriate learning platforms and tools, providing guidelines and resources for navigating the virtual learning environment, and offering timely technical assistance to address any issues that may arise during the learning process.

Monitoring and Evaluation: Assessing the effectiveness of virtual learning initiatives can be more challenging in remote work settings. L&D professionals should employ a combination of evaluation methods, such as surveys, quizzes, and analytics, to gauge learner progress, satisfaction, and the overall impact of the training program. This data can then be used to refine and improve future learning initiatives.

Remote Work Skills Development: In addition to traditional training topics, L&D professionals should also focus on developing the specific skills and competencies required for remote work success. This may include training on time management, virtual communication, self-motivation, and the effective use of digital tools and platforms.

By addressing the unique challenges and opportunities of remote work, L&D professionals can design and deliver virtual learning experiences that are engaging, effective, and accessible to a widely dispersed workforce. This will enable organizations to continue fostering a culture of continuous learning and development, even as the nature of work continues to evolve.

1.6 THE INCREASING IMPORTANCE OF AGILITY AND ADAPTABILITY

L&D professionals have a pivotal role in nurturing agility and adaptability within their workforce, helping employees develop the skills and mindset necessary to thrive in an uncertain environment. One way of achieving this is by incorporating adaptability intelligence (AQ) into their learning and development programs.

Adaptability intelligence, as developed by AQai, focuses on an individual's ability to adjust and thrive in different situations and environments. By measuring and improving AQ, organizations can foster a workforce that is more resilient, flexible, and innovative. AQai has built the world's largest community of certified AQ coaches, consultants, and professionals, who are equipped with the tools and knowledge to help organizations assess and enhance their employees' adaptability.

Adaptability is a huge subject. Indeed, there are seventeen subdimensions on the Adaptiotic table. This can be overwhelming when contemplating incorporating AQ and adaptability intelligence into your learning and development programs. Thus, before we deep dive into AQ, we have identified three key places you could start.

Firstly, one of the key aspects of fostering agility and adaptability is cultivating **resilience** among employees, which is an essential component of adaptability intelligence. L&D professionals can develop training programs that help individuals build mental and emotional resilience by teaching coping strategies, stress management techniques, and problem-solving skills.

Another crucial element in promoting adaptability is nurturing a **growth mindset** within the organization, which is closely related to AQ. A growth mindset encourages individuals to embrace challenges, learn from their mistakes, and continuously seek opportunities for self-improvement. L&D professionals can foster a growth mindset and improve AQ by incorporating training programs that emphasize the value of learning from setbacks, provide constructive feedback, and celebrate progress and personal growth.

Finally, the shift in employees' working and learning requirements calls for a more dynamic and real-time approach to learning and development. L&D professionals must adapt their strategies to cater to these evolving needs, offering flexible and on-demand learning experiences that allow employees to access training when and where it is most relevant to them. By leveraging technology and innovative learning platforms, L&D professionals can deliver personalized and engaging learning experiences that support employees in their ongoing development and help improve their adaptability intelligence.

By partnering with organizations like AQai and leveraging the expertise of their certified AQ coaches and professionals, L&D professionals can equip employees with the skills and mindset necessary to navigate the complexities and uncertainties of today's business world. This will ultimately lead to a more innovative, adaptable, and successful organization, capable of thriving in the face of change.

We'll cover practical ways to foster AQ in your learning and development programs in section 1.9.

A Deeper dive

As we explore the concept of **Adaptability Quotient (AQ)**, a groundbreaking approach to understanding and enhancing an organization's ability to adapt and respond to change. At the heart of **AQ is the A.C.E. model**, which encompasses three core dimensions of adaptability: **Ability, Character, and Environment.** By analysing and optimizing these dimensions, businesses can cultivate the resilience, agility, and innovation necessary for success in an unpredictable and complex world.

We have spent years collating the highest level of peer-reviewed studies, established research, and cutting-edge trends to create a comprehensive operating system for adaptability. The A.C.E. model offers a comprehensive framework for assessing and developing adaptability within organizations. The three dimensions of adaptability are as follows:

Our understanding of AQ is based on three interrelated inputs, or master dimensions, which are:

AQ Ability (your adaptability skills - How and to what degree one adapts)

This dimension represents your adaptation muscle system. It reflects how you can develop mastery in multiple or changing fields over time. This element encompasses your ability to be resilient and bounce back—or even forward—from hardship, mental flexibility in holding opposing thoughts, grit, mindset, and the ability to unlearn.

AQ Character (who adapts and why)

This dimension reflects the more innate (but contextual) aspect of adaptability quotient, broadly described as "the way you tick." It includes what drives you, your frames of mind, and your working styles. This master dimension uncovers your profile in motivation style, emotional range, extraversion, thinking style, and hope.

AQ Environment (how your environment can help or hinder your adaption - When one adapts, and to what degree)

Your environment can either help or inhibit your adaptation. This dimension explores areas such as company support, team support (psychological safety), work environment, emotional health, and work stress.

These three master dimensions further break down into seventeen sub-dimensions, which allows us to drill down into specifics, creating what we call our **"AQ Adaptiotic Table™."**

THE A.C.E MODEL OF ADAPTABILITY

THE 17 SCIENTIFICALLY VALID MEASURES OF ADAPTABILITY

THE AQ ADAPTIOTIC™ TABLE

AQ ABILITY

HOW AND TO WHAT DEGREE DO I ADAPT?

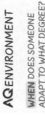

1. GRIT
2. MENTAL FLEXIBILITY
3. MINDSET
4. RESILIENCE
5. UNLEARN

AQ CHARACTER

WHO ADAPTS AND WHY?

6. EMOTIONAL RANGE
7. EXTRAVERSION
8. HOPE
9. MOTIVATION STYLE
10. THINKING STYLE

AQ ENVIRONMENT

WHEN DOES SOMEONE ADAPT TO WHAT DEGREE?

11. COMPANY SUPPORT
12. EMOTIONAL HEALTH
13. TEAM SUPPORT
14. WORK ENVIRONMENT
15. WORK STRESS

AI PREDICTIVE INDEXES

16. CHANGE READINESS INDEX
17. RESKILL INDEX

THE AQ GUY

AQai.

Collaborating with Dr. Nicholas T. Deuschel, a research professor at Spain's leading Carlos III University, we utilized one of the most robust models in organizational psychology (the input-process-outcome model) to create our tripartite Ability Character Environment model (or A.C.E.). In our model, "adaptability" is the outcome, a result of a process and an input.

In our A.C.E. model, AQ-Character fuels adaptation (the "input"), meaning that traits such as extraversion-introversion, motivation style, and "personality traits" create the impetus that drives us to adapt. Building on dozens of studies in psychology and business, as well as our research, we have found that while certain character types may be more innately adaptable, AQ-Character establishes why we adapt in the first place.

Moreover, employees can learn new skills that allow them to adapt in different ways, adding to the "input" stage of the model. This is AQ-Ability.

Additionally, we are influenced by our environment. We may possess unique skills and an innately adaptable personality, but due to an inhibiting environment, we might be unable to fully harness our AQ potential. This is another critical "input."

The "process" stage involves adaptability behaviors such as exploration (seeking out new ideas and ways of doing things), exploitation (utilizing and maximizing current resources and approaches), problem-solving, and creativity. In a business context, these manifest in a series of outputs, including desired, predicted, and actual "outcomes." Examples of outcomes are accelerated innovation, employee engagement, retention and reskilling, increased employee mobility and dynamic career pathways, a learning and development culture, overall productivity and performance, and improved health and wellbeing, such as reduced stress and burnout.

Understanding the specific flow, mix, and value of inputs, the resulting and chosen processes, and the impact on outcomes helps us continually leverage and optimize our adaptability intelligence. It is also essential to consider the loop effect, where many 'outputs' become feedback data points as future inputs. This comprehensive understanding of AQ and its benefits for businesses can lead to improved adaptability, growth, and success in a rapidly changing world.

1.7 THE SCIENCE OF ADAPTABILITY

We used one of the most robust models in organisational psychology (the input-process-outcome model) to create our tripartite **Ability Character Environment** model (or A.C.E.). In our case "adaptability" is the outcome, a result of a process and an input.

In our model, AQ-Character catalysts adaption (this is the "input"). In other words extraversion-introversion, our motivation style, our "personality traits", all create the impetus that drives us to adapt.

At the same time employees can learn new skills that allow them to adapt in different ways. This is AQ-Ability which also adds to the "input" stage of the model.

In addition, we are also influenced by our environment. We may have all the unique skills in the world to help us adapt, even a personality that is innately adaptable, but due to an inhibiting environment are unable to fully harness our AQ muscle. This is also another important "input".

INPUT

AQ ABILITY
GRIT
MENTAL FLEXIBILITY
MINDSET
RESILIENCE
UNLEARN

AQ CHARACTER
EMOTIONAL RANGE
EXTRAVERSION
HOPE
MOTIVATION STYLE
THINKING STYLE

AQ ENVIRONMENT
COMPANY SUPPORT
EMOTIONAL HEALTH
TEAM SUPPORT
WORK ENVIRONMENT
WORK STRESS

PROCESS

ADAPTABILITY BEHAVIOURS

EXPLORE & TRANSFORM
EXPLOITATION - UTILIZE & IMPROVE
PROBLEM-SOLVING
CREATIVITY
COMMUNICATION LEVELS
LEADERSHIP STYLES
PRACTICES & PROCEDURES
SPEED OF LEARNING
DECISION MAKING
PRO-ACTIVE
REACTIVE

OUTPUT

ACCELERATED INNOVATION
PROFITABILITY
RELEVANCE
EMPLOYEE ENGAGEMENT
RETENTION
RESKILLING
EMPLOYEE MOBILITY
DYNAMIC CAREER PATHWAYS
LEARNING AND DEVELOPMENT
CULTURE
PRODUCTIVITY & PERFORMANCE
MENTAL HEALTH
WELLBEING, STRESS, BURNOUT
COLLAPSE / THRIVING

EXAMPLES OF THE INPUT, PROCESS, OUTPUT MODEL
IN RELATION TO ADAPTABILITY

Ross Thornley THE AQ GUY

AQai

Of course, this is only scratching the surface. But hopefully this basic overview has given you an idea of how the underlying principles of AQ are present and active in our lives.

What would you do differently looking at your team and business within the context of the three master dimensions?

1.8 THE NEW SKILLS AND COMPETENCIES FOR L&D PROFESSIONALS

To thrive in their evolving roles, L&D professionals must develop a range of new skills and competencies, some of the main ones include:

> → **ADAPTABILITY:** BEING ABLE TO QUICKLY ADJUST TO CHANGES IN THE BUSINESS ENVIRONMENT AND ADAPT LEARNING PROGRAMS ACCORDINGLY
>
> → **STRATEGIC THINKING:** UNDERSTANDING THE ORGANIZATION'S GOALS AND ALIGNING L&D INITIATIVES WITH THESE OBJECTIVES.
>
> → **DATA-DRIVEN DECISION MAKING:** LEVERAGING LEARNING ANALYTICS AND OTHER DATA SOURCES TO INFORM THE DESIGN, IMPLEMENTATION, AND EVALUATION OF L&D PROGRAMS.
>
> → **TECHNOLOGICAL PROFICIENCY:** STAYING

UP-TO-DATE WITH EMERGING TECHNOLOGIES AND
INCORPORATING THEM INTO LEARNING SOLUTIONS.

→ **COLLABORATION AND COMMUNICATION:**
WORKING EFFECTIVELY WITH STAKEHOLDERS ACROSS
THE ORGANIZATION TO SUPPORT LEARNING AND
PERFORMANCE IMPROVEMENT.

By developing these skills and competencies, L&D professionals can position themselves as strategic partners within their organizations, driving growth and success in the age of rapid change.

In the following chapters, we will delve deeper into how L&D professionals can embrace adaptability, leverage technology, and design future-ready learning programs that support the growth and development of their workforce.

1.9 THE SHIFT FROM EXPERIENCE TO EXPERIMENTATION & SPEED OF LEARNING

Traditionally, organizations have relied on experience as a predictor of future success, valuing employees with extensive knowledge and a proven track record in their respective fields. However, in an era of constant change and disruption, relying solely on experience is no longer sufficient. The ability to experiment, learn quickly, and adapt has become an essential quality for both individuals and organizations.

L&D professionals must now focus on cultivating a culture of experimentation within their organizations, encouraging employees to test new ideas, learn from their failures, and iterate on their successes. This shift also requires L&D professionals to prioritize speed of learning, designing programs that enable employees to acquire new skills and knowledge rapidly, and apply them in real-time to stay ahead of the competition.

To support this shift, L&D professionals should consider incorporating the following elements into their learning programs:

Emphasize a Growth Mindset:

Encouraging employees to adopt a growth mindset necessitates promoting an environment where challenges are welcomed, and mistakes are seen as opportunities for learning rather than failures. You can facilitate this by setting up regular feedback sessions where employees can discuss their challenges and learnings. In addition, recognizing and rewarding effort, improvement, and resilience instead of just performance can signal your commitment to fostering a growth mindset. You can further bolster this mindset by providing learning resources and professional development opportunities that focus on improvement and lifelong learning.

Foster a Culture of Innovation:

Cultivating a culture of innovation requires more than merely encouraging employees to think creatively. It calls for creating an environment where cross-functional collaboration and idea-sharing are the norms. Consider establishing innovation labs or hackathons where employees across different functions can collaborate on new ideas or solutions. Additionally, make sure to recognize and celebrate innovative ideas and solutions, regardless of whether they are successfully implemented. This signals that risk-taking and experimentation are valued and can motivate employees to think out of the box.

Implement Agile Learning Methodologies:

The implementation of agile learning methodologies involves adopting a flexible, iterative, and learner-centric approach to learning program design and delivery. This could be achieved by using methods like microlearning, which breaks down complex concepts into bite-sized modules, allowing for easier absorption and retention. Moreover, using blended learning strategies, combining digital and face-to-face delivery methods, can provide flexibility and cater to different learning styles. Consider providing learners with personalized learning paths that adapt to their progress, areas of strength, and areas for improvement.

Measure Learning Outcomes:

The effective measurement of learning outcomes relies on the systematic collection and analysis of data from learning initiatives. Start by determining the key performance indicators (KPIs) that align with your learning objectives. These could include knowledge acquisition, behavior change, or impact on business results. Once these KPIs are established, use learning analytics tools to collect data and track these indicators over time. Ensure to communicate the outcomes and insights gained from these analyses to relevant stakeholders. This information can inform future program design and highlight areas for improvement, illustrating the importance and effectiveness of your learning initiatives.

1.10 THE IMPACT OF CHATGPT-4 ON DIGITAL LEARNING

The introduction of advanced language models like ChatGPT-4 has further revolutionized the world of digital learning. ChatGPT-4, developed by OpenAI, is an AI-powered language model capable of generating human-like text based on context and user input. Its capabilities have opened up new opportunities for L&D professionals to enhance learning experiences and engage learners more effectively.

The impact of ChatGPT-4 on digital learning includes:

→ **PERSONALIZED LEARNING:** CHATGPT-4 CAN BE USED TO DEVELOP TAILORED LEARNING CONTENT AND RESOURCES BASED ON INDIVIDUAL LEARNER PREFERENCES, NEEDS, AND GOALS. THIS ENABLES L&D PROFESSIONALS TO CREATE MORE RELEVANT AND ENGAGING LEARNING EXPERIENCES.

→ **INTERACTIVE LEARNING:** CHATGPT-4 CAN BE INTEGRATED INTO LEARNING PLATFORMS TO PROVIDE REAL-TIME, AI-DRIVEN FEEDBACK AND SUPPORT, ALLOWING LEARNERS TO ASK QUESTIONS, RECEIVE GUIDANCE, AND DISCUSS CONCEPTS IN A MORE INTERACTIVE AND ENGAGING MANNER.

→ **LEARNING ANALYTICS:** CHATGPT-4 CAN BE USED TO ANALYZE LEARNER DATA, SUCH AS PROGRESS, PERFORMANCE, AND ENGAGEMENT, HELPING L&D PROFESSIONALS MAKE DATA-DRIVEN DECISIONS TO IMPROVE LEARNING OUTCOMES.

→ **CONTENT CREATION:** L&D PROFESSIONALS CAN LEVERAGE CHATGPT-4 TO GENERATE CONTENT FOR VARIOUS LEARNING MATERIALS, SUCH AS ARTICLES, CASE STUDIES, AND QUIZZES, SAVING TIME AND RESOURCES.

By incorporating ChatGPT-4 into their digital learning strategies, L&D professionals can offer more engaging, personalized, and effective learning experiences, ultimately driving higher levels of learner satisfaction and performance improvement.

CHAPTER 2: BUILDING YOUR OWN PERSONAL ADAPTABILITY

Personal adaptability is about your ability to unlearn, re-lean at speed, and respond effectively to change. Doing so will you to navigate the complexities of the evolving L&D landscape with ease and provide an important role model for other in your organization.

To build your personal adaptability, an easy first step is to begin by cultivating a mindset of openness and curiosity. Truly welcome new experiences and be prepared to step outside your own comfort zone, even better do this in a public setting! Regularly engage with new concepts, technologies, and methodologies within and outside of the L&D industry to expand your own horizons, imagination and inspiration.

You will no doubt already consider your professional development as an ongoing journey and not a destination. Continuous learning is integral to personal adaptability, so don't forget to seek out opportunities for your own professional growth. Attending webinars, workshops, or conferences is a super simple way to do this. I advise scheduling this out in your calendar every 90 days, and include at least one session a month; enroll in relevant (and maybe even seemingly irrelevant) courses; and consider pursuing additional qualifications.

2.1 CULTIVATING A GROWTH MINDSET

A growth mindset, as conceptualized by psychologist Carol Dweck, involves viewing challenges as opportunities for learning, embracing the potential for personal and professional evolution, and understanding that abilities and intelligence can be developed.

To nurture this mindset, consciously challenge any fixed beliefs you hold about your own skills and capabilities. When you encounter obstacles, view them as opportunities for growth. Acknowledge your missteps as necessary steps towards mastery, and celebrate your progress, no matter how small.

Seek and accept feedback from your peers, superiors, and learners, viewing it as valuable information to improve your performance. Praise the effort and strategies you use in your work, not just the outcomes. This can help reinforce your belief in the possibility of development and improvement.

I'd like to share an excerpt from my Decoding AQ book

here. About reacting and responding.

2.2 RE-MODEL FROM REACT TO RESPOND

It is often said that knowledge is power, but knowledge alone cannot change the world. We have to use that knowledge. In this chapter, I want to move from thinking to planning (which is the first stage of action!).

When facing uncertainty, one of our most basic and in-built reactions is to seek more knowledge, and more data, to help us combat our uncertainty—to move from the unknown to the known. It's a deeply ingrained pattern in us.

The greater the change, the more energy (and data) we require. "Hence, paradoxically, as we accumulate more data and increase our computing power, events become wilder and more unexpected."

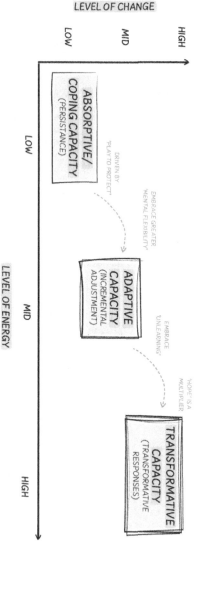

THE GREATER THE CHANGE REQUIRED
THE MORE ENERGY WE NEED

SUSTAINING OUR ENERGY & RESOURCES TO CONTINUALLY CHANGE BEGINS WITH RECOGNIZING THE DIFFERENT
CAPACITIES WE HAVE, AND THE REPLENISHMENT TO CHANGE WITHOUT DESTRUCTION, BURNOUT OR BREAKDOWN.

LEVEL OF CHANGE

HIGH
MID
LOW

ABSORPTIVE/
COPING CAPACITY
(PERSISTANCE)

DRIVEN BY
'PLAY TO PROTECT'

EMBRACE GREATER
'MENTAL FLEXIBILITY'

ADAPTIVE
CAPACITY
(INCREMENTAL
ADJUSTMENT)

EMBRACE
'UNLEARNING'

'HOPE' IS A
MULTIPLIER

TRANSFORMATIVE
CAPACITY
(TRANSFORMATIVE
RESPONSES)

LEVEL OF ENERGY

LOW   MID   HIGH

THE AQ GUY

SOURCE: INSPIRED FROM WILEY.COM

AQai.

We can observe this process in even simple and day-to-day activities. If we want to travel somewhere, for example, we look up the route. If it's somewhere we don't visit frequently, we might also have concerns about traffic, so we'll look at the road reports or check Google Maps. We might even check the weather forecast. When we are in a relaxed and open mind frame, rather than an amygdala hijack, we use this data to create a plan. We choose to avoid certain roads. We map out our route. And we bring contingencies for the weather, such as an umbrella.

However, when we are in a fear state, and the amygdala is "in the driver's seat", no amount of data can actually help us. We can, in fact, suffer from "data overload" where we get stuck in a loop of consuming more and more information, believing that somehow it will solve our problem or alleviate our uncertainty, whereas actually each new piece of information only adds to our concern!

We need only look at Covid-19 as an easy example of this. During the height of lockdown, many of us were glued to our TV screens, watching the news, fed a daily meal of disaster, scary numbers, and new frightening research on the virus, and none of it helped us move from uncertainty to certainty, it only added to the fear! Likewise, in a business environment, with so much change happening, we can feel paralysed. We want to remove the paralysis by getting more information about this new "threat" we perceive, whether it's a "competitor", a disruption, an economic factor, or even an environmental problem. However, we have to recognise when to move from gathering data about a transformative event to creating a plan based on the information we have and trying to move forward.

There is a correlation between the size of the transformation event and the amount of data we think we require. In the previous example of bad weather and traffic on the roads, we need very little additional information to pivot our strategy. However, when a streaming service has rendered our brick-and-mortar store redundant, and our whole business model is overturned, we require much more information to deal with it! In fact, we might feel we require more information than perhaps possible for a human being to readily compute, which is why we have to begin moving forward, begin planning, and acting, even though we won't have all the answers at hand.

To do this, we need to find the right balance between **reacting** to problems and **responding** to them. This is because craving more data is *itself a reaction*, not a response. And worse, it can become an addiction too!

A *reaction* is automatic. When a bird swoops overhead, we duck. This is an innate, virtually genetic survival instinct that is in all of us. Sadly, these survival instincts—these automatic muscle-memory reactions—can play havoc with us as we try to navigate an ever-shifting exponential world. If every time we perceive ourselves to be threatened we either "duck" or "attack", we quickly alienate everyone around us.

There are several large corporations that recently posted massive losses because customers have become disillusioned by the way these organisations have treated smaller creators using their IP. Large corporations view suing others as protecting their interests, but when legal action starts to hurt people who are genuinely enthused about your product, people who are promoting your product for free (some coaches call these "super fans" for how they become walking advertisements of your product or service), it's a very ugly look indeed. The corporations who have instead *leveraged* the people enthused about their IP, on the other hand, are seeing massive wins.

This reminds me of a story once told to me by a friend of mine with an unusual background, given his current role; he was a school teacher for many years before becoming a coach, trainer, and entrepreneur (unusual, although no doubt that gives one a lot of insight into psychology and what is really motivating people from an early age). He was a drama teacher and was putting on a play in which he wanted to use the music of Paul Simon. Though he probably was being overly cautious, he called Paul Simon's agent and asked if they would be allowed to use the song in the school production. Simon's agent flatly refused and said they would sue the school if they went ahead and used the song anyway. My friend then called up the BeeGees' agent. The agent laughed at the very idea of a school teacher asking permission to use a song in a school play. The agent said that the BeeGees loved it when they heard about people using their material creatively and considered it a compliment. My friend concludes the story with a wry remark: "To my knowledge, the BeeGees have sold a fair few more records than Paul Simon." Indeed, they have sold approximately 213 million more! The generosity of spirit goes a long way. The BeeGees were not *threatened* by someone using their IP. They instead responded, recognising that all of this was simply a free promotion for them. To reiterate and emphasise my point here: the ability to be generous, rather than controlling and defensive, **comes from a responsive not a reactive place**. If we dwell in a reactive state, we won't be able to harness our giving and generous side.

In order to give a response, rather than succumbing to a reaction, we must harness "the pulse of adaptive behaviour". This "pulse" might be considered a deep breath, a pause. It is a moment where we step back rather than allowing the muscle memory of our in-built responses to take over.

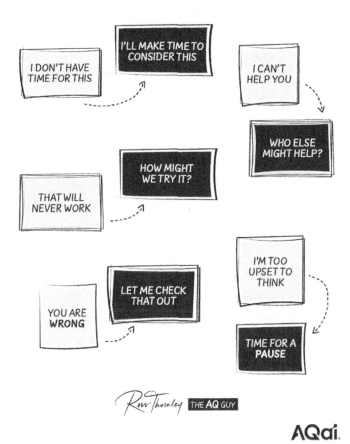

2.3 THE FOUR RS

A daptive pulses are also about taking in the context of a situation. Had my friend been producing a play on the West End, then the response might have been different. It might have been perfectly reasonable for the BeeGees to have asked for a licensing fee for the use of their song. But the context was a school play.

Our society is, sadly, largely geared towards competition and avoidance of loss. This means we have a tendency to focus on short-term wins. As David Green observes: "Too many short-term performance goals focused on results and outputs can lead to an overly competitive environment where burnout and one-upmanship pervade. Balancing these short-term goals with long-term goals focused on learning, mastery and the journey being taken will help to keep perspective and create an environment of greater collaboration, trust and sense of growth."

I think of this as "zooming in and zooming out". In the corporate world, this tends to have the meaning of "big picture" thinking versus "detail". However, I think it is more useful to consider vantage points. What vantage points can we leverage to help us imaginatively? Rather than thirsting for data, can we move to a place of empathetic vision in which we see the so-called "problem" from an entirely different perspective?

When we're driving a car and we want to change gears, before we can shift into the next gear, we have to disengage the motion source, and go via "neutral". Going into neutral is in some ways quite scary because the car is in a state of undefined direction in neutral. And if we stay in neutral too long, we'll most certainly never get anywhere! However, without neutral, we cannot get anywhere else—forwards or backwards—we cannot shift gears.

Another term I use for this is "limbo". When we receive external stimuli we deem to be threatening, or when we enter the unknown, our minds and bodies, like a car, realise that they need to shift gear, and we need to enter a moment of neutral or limbo. Ken Wilber described this phenomenon in a fascinating analogy:

"For instance, if I come up behind you and yell 'Boo!' there will be a few seconds wherein you remain still, even though you have heard me yell, and during this very brief time **you might feel a type of passive or quiet alertness**, but this feeling shortly explodes into a sensation of mild shock (or something similar) accompanied with an onrush of thoughts and emotions… **In those few seconds of passive awareness, your Energy was beginning to mobilize but it was not yet experienced as shock or mild terror**–it was pure and without form, and only later did it disintegrate into thoughts and emotions of shock and fright."

In other words, there is a moment before our reaction becomes manifest where we occupy a completely detached, objective, and unbiased vantage point whereby we can truly assess the correct response to a given stimulus. This limbo, then, is a realm of immense potential, especially when we consider that adaptability, "is the capacity to adjust one's thoughts and behaviours in order to effectively respond to uncertainty, new information, or changed circumstances."[4] By *leaning in* to this moment of limbo, by leaning into the pause, we can head off our reaction and instead craft a *response* with considered thought and action.

2.4 THE FOUR RS TO TRANSFORM SETBACKS INTO SPRINGBOARDS

To transition from "reaction" to "response" we can use my process of the Four Rs.

→ 1. RECOGNISE. THIS CORRELATES TO WHAT WE DISCUSSED EARLIER ABOUT SIMPLY OBSERVING, DECOUPLING FROM OUR EMOTIONS AND TAKING IN THE SITUATION WITHOUT FEELING THE NEED TO IDENTIFY WITH A SENSE OF FAILURE OR DESPAIR. THIS IS ENTERING "LIMBO" OR "NEUTRAL".

→ 2. REFLECT. ONCE WE HAVE TAKEN A MOMENT OF PAUSE TO "RECOGNISE" THE REALITY OF THE

SITUATION, WE CAN MORE OBJECTIVELY "REFLECT" ON WHAT STEPS LED US TO THIS MOMENT OF SETBACK, WE CAN CONSIDER NEW INFORMATION, NOW IN AN ENHANCED COGNITIVE STATE.

→ 3. RE-IMAGINE. NOW, ARMED WITH VALUABLE KNOWLEDGE, WE CAN LOOK FORWARD INSTEAD OF BACK. WHAT NEW DOORS ARE AVAILABLE TO US? HOW CAN WE RE-IMAGINE OUR PARADIGM, OUR METHODOLOGY, OUR STRATEGY, OUR PROCESS, OUR WHATEVER—AND TURN THE SITUATION AROUND?

→ 4. RESPOND. NOW WE CAN TAKE DELIBERATE AND INTENTIONAL STEPS TOWARD NEW OPPORTUNITIES.

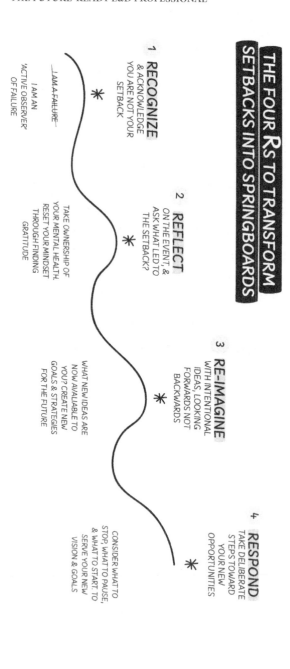

THE FOUR Rs TO TRANSFORM
SETBACKS INTO SPRINGBOARDS

1 RECOGNIZE
& ACKNOWLEDGE
YOU ARE NOT YOUR
SETBACK

I AM A FAILURE

I AM AN
'ACTIVE OBSERVER'
OF FAILURE

2 REFLECT
ON THE EVENT, &
ASK WHAT LED TO
THE SETBACK?

TAKE OWNERSHIP OF
YOUR MENTAL HEALTH.
RESET YOUR MINDSET
THROUGH FINDING
GRATITUDE

3 RE-IMAGINE
WITH INTENTIONAL
IDEAS, LOOKING
FORWARDS NOT
BACKWARDS

WHAT NEW IDEAS ARE
NOW AVAILABLE TO
YOU? CREATE NEW
GOALS & STRATEGIES
FOR THE FUTURE

4 RESPOND
TAKE DELIBERATE
STEPS TOWARD
YOUR NEW
OPPORTUNITIES

CONSIDER WHAT TO
STOP, WHAT TO PAUSE,
& WHAT TO START, TO
SERVE YOUR NEW
VISION & GOALS

THE AQ GUY

AQai.

Of course, it is not easy to decouple from our emotions, nor is it easy to pause and observe events without becoming emotionally invested. By definition "limbo" is a scary place because it is neutral, because we do not see the familiar reminders and confirmations of our existing paradigms. This correlates with Mental Flexibility, or what Keats called "Negative Capability" and F. Scott Fitzgerald's praised as "the ability to hold two opposed ideas in mind at the same time and still retain the ability to function." It is in this "limbo" state, before *reaction*, that we can hold the multiple polarities in mind and decide consciously upon the right course. It is essential we learn to harness this power to enhance our adaptability intelligence.

Embracing alternative viewpoints correlates to step 2 of harnessing our AQ potential as leaders. Here is a handy summary that will show you where you may or may not be maximising this faculty:

SIGNS YOU MIGHT NOT BE MAXIMIZING YOUR ADAPTABILITY INTELLIGENCE

LANGUISHING IN A PLACE OF COMFORT OR FRUSTRATION, PARALYZES YOU FROM YOUR WORK AND LIFE. RECOGNIZE UNHEALTHY THOUGHTS, BEHAVIOURS AND PATTERNS, AND CREATE NEW, MORE PRODUCTIVE HABITS.

1   ONLY LISTENING TO ONE NEWS CHANNEL

2   SHALLOW BREATHING

3   LIMITING YOUR GOALS, BASED ON YOUR PAST

4   NOT CHALLENGING OTHERS, FOR FEAR OF CONFLICT

5   TOLERATING AN UNSUPPORTIVE ENVIRONMENT

Ross Thornley   THE **AQ** GUY

AQai.

Businesses tend to understand the world through two lenses: people who make what exists better, and people who imagine (and create) what doesn't exist. The paradox that we must embrace using Mental Flexibility is of course that we need to be doing both concurrently. The improvement of the old does not invalidate the creation of the new and vice-versa. However, we also have to recognise that existing within this paradox can be very draining. As we saw from the example by Ken Wilber, our responses *disperse* our mobilised energy. So, choosing a conscious, considered response costs us more energy than allowing muscle memory to take over. This is partly why muscle memory and automatic/involuntary reactions exist—as an efficiency. This is correlated with biology. If you want to make significant muscle gains, the worst thing you can do is the same routine every day. The muscles, tendons, and nervous system quickly acclimate to the familiar stresses and learn "shortcuts" that ease the load on the body. Therefore, the amount of benefit you gain from the training is a law of diminishing returns. Top trainers challenge their athletes with new and different exercises every single day so that their bodies cannot fall into this automatic and familiar routine. Our minds are the same!

VARIATION IS TO BE WELCOMED, NOT REJECTED AND FEARED.

In the world of work, we tend to imagine all processes and efforts as being regular, even, and balanced. The phrase "work/ life" balance has permeated our everyday communications. As business owners, we are expected to increase profits by a predictable percentage each year. If we are not "growing" all the time, then surely we're dying? And so on. But the reality is that life moves in cycles and rhythms. We'll explore this in more detail later on, but for now, we can simply look at the "pulse of adaption".

The pulse of adaption is not just about the individual response and taking a pause before reacting to a situation. **It also operates at the organisational level.** As businesses, we must **build "pulses of adaption" into our work cycles.**

Rather than aiming for extreme levels of concentrated effort over extended periods of time, it is more realistic to attempt sprints of heightened effort that are then followed by a pulse, a pause, where we can assess what we've done, what the projections are, and where we might need to pivot. This manner of working might resemble a heartbeat. There is a rising peak of mental effort and concentration followed by a dip, a valley. This is the natural rhythm of existence. That is a business. That is life.

A PERFECTLY EVEN AND BALANCED FLATLINE IS, OF COURSE, DEATH!

By planning these moments of pause into your project lifecycle, and relinquishing the rigidity of "sticking to the plan", you will set yourself and your team up for success by becoming agile, adaptable, and *responsive* rather than "always-on" and *reactive*.

If this chapter resonated, please checkout the complete book **DECODING AQ YOUR GREATEST SUPERPOWER - A new Operating Stsyem For Change In An Exponential World.**

CHAPTER 3: ADAPTING TO NON-DEDICATED L&D RESOURCES

Role of HR Leaders in L&D:

In smaller organizations or those without a dedicated L&D department, HR leaders often wear multiple hats, including overseeing L&D functions. Such a role requires strategic alignment of employee development with broader HR strategies like talent acquisition, employee retention, and performance management. HR leaders can seamlessly integrate L&D functions into their role, focusing on areas such as understanding the training needs of employees, facilitating knowledge sharing, and finding easy ways to promote a learning culture within the organization.

HR leaders can effectively take on L&D functions by first identifying the specific needs of their organization. This could involve employee surveys, performance reviews, or direct consultations. Based on these needs, they can then outline clear learning objectives and design or source appropriate training programs. To ensure learning is continuous, they should also encourage peer-to-peer learning and knowledge sharing within teams. As an HR leader in this situation, maintain open lines of communication with employees to keep abreast of their learning needs.

Consider how might you better integrate L&D into your current HR role, and what steps can you take to enhance a learning culture within your organization?

Building L&D Skills within HR:

For HR professionals who find themselves tasked with L&D responsibilities, building core competencies in key areas can dramatically enhance their effectiveness. A a simple starter, these include skills such as conducting a needs assessment to identify knowledge gaps, designing and developing effective training programs, assessing the impact of training initiatives on performance, and staying updated with emerging L&D trends and technologies. Why not try an experiment with ChatGPT to see how you can develop new training programs, and create need assessments.

CHAPTER 4: DESIGNING FUTURE-READY LEARNING PROGRAMS

4.1 IDENTIFYING KEY SKILLS FOR THE FUTURE OF WORK

As the world of work evolves, L&D professionals must stay ahead of emerging trends to ensure their organizations are equipped with the skills needed for future success. This chapter will explore how to identify the most critical skills for the future of work, including:

> → **SOFT SKILLS/HUMAN SKILLS:** EXAMINING THE GROWING IMPORTANCE OF HUMAN SKILLS SUCH AS ADAPTABILITY, EMOTIONAL INTELLIGENCE, COLLABORATION, AND CREATIVE PROBLEM-SOLVING.
>
> → **TECHNICAL SKILLS:** DISCUSSING THE IMPORTANCE OF STAYING UP-TO-DATE WITH TECHNOLOGY TRENDS AND THE LATEST TOOLS AND PLATFORMS RELEVANT TO YOUR INDUSTRY.
>
> → **LEARNING AGILITY:** EXPLORING HOW LEARNING AGILITY, OR THE ABILITY TO LEARN AND APPLY NEW SKILLS QUICKLY, HAS BECOME A CRITICAL SKILL IN THE MODERN WORKPLACE.

4.2 HUMAN SKILLS - CREATING A CULTURE OF LIFELONG LEARNING

A culture of lifelong learning is vital for organizations to maintain a competitive edge and ensure employees are continuously developing and refining their skills. L&D professionals play a critical role in fostering this culture, which requires strategic planning, commitment, and support from various stakeholders within the organization. This chapter outlines strategies for creating a culture of lifelong learning, focusing on leadership support, diverse learning opportunities, and recognition and rewards.

Leadership support is crucial to the success of any life-long learning initiative. When organizational leaders demonstrate their commitment to continuous learning, employees are more likely to embrace and prioritize their professional development. L&D professionals should work closely with leaders to communicate the value and benefits of lifelong learning, ensuring they serve as role models by actively participating in learning opportunities themselves. Additionally, leaders should be involved in the design and delivery of learning programs, providing resources, time, and support to enable employee development.

Offering diverse learning opportunities is another essential aspect of cultivating a culture of lifelong learning. L&D professionals should provide a range of options that cater to different learning styles, preferences, and needs. This can include workshops, online courses, on-the-job training, mentorship programs, and more. By leveraging technology and innovative learning platforms, L&D professionals can deliver personalized, engaging, and effective learning experiences. For instance, using adaptive learning technologies, employees can receive customized content and recommendations based on their learning progress, ensuring they remain engaged and motivated throughout the learning process.

Recognition and rewards play a significant role in incentivizing continuous development among employees. By implementing systems to acknowledge and reward learning achievements, L&D professionals can encourage employees to take ownership of their professional growth. This can involve setting up a digital badging system, where employees earn badges for completing courses or achieving specific learning milestones. Alternatively, L&D professionals can establish a reward system tied to performance reviews, where employees who demonstrate a commitment to continuous learning receive additional benefits, such as promotions or bonuses.

Creating a culture of lifelong learning is essential for organizations to maintain a competitive edge and support the continuous development of their workforce. L&D professionals must secure leadership support, offer diverse learning opportunities, and implement recognition and reward systems to foster a learning culture. By doing so, they can empower employees to take charge of their professional growth, resulting in a more skilled, adaptable, and motivated workforce, ready to tackle the challenges of an ever-changing business landscape.

4.3 TECHNICAL SKILLS - INTEGRATING EMERGING TECHNOLOGIES INTO LEARNING PROGRAMS

As technology continues to advance at a rapid pace, L&D professionals must stay informed about the latest tools and platforms that can enhance the learning experience for their employees. This chapter will discuss how to integrate emerging technologies, such as virtual reality (VR), augmented reality (AR), and AI-driven learning platforms, into your learning programs, and explore strategies for assessing suitability, piloting, evaluating, and supporting employees in using new learning technologies.

Before integrating any new technology into a learning program, L&D professionals must first assess its suitability for their organization's learning needs. This involves identifying the specific challenges and objectives that the technology aims to address, as well as evaluating its potential impact on employee engagement, skill development, and performance outcomes. L&D professionals should also consider factors such as cost, scalability, and compatibility with existing systems when determining the feasibility of adopting a new technology.

Once a suitable technology has been identified, the next step is to pilot and evaluate its effectiveness within the learning program. L&D professionals should design small-scale pilot programs, incorporating the new technology into a specific training module or course. This allows them to gather feedback from employees, identify potential issues or barriers to adoption, and assess the technology's impact on learning outcomes. Based on the results of the pilot program, L&D professionals can then make informed decisions about whether to scale up the technology's implementation and integrate it more widely into the organization's learning initiatives.

Integrating emerging technologies into learning programs also requires training and support for employees who will be using these new tools. L&D professionals should develop training materials and resources to help employees understand the purpose and functionality of the new technology, as well as providing guidance on how to use it effectively within their learning journey. This can include creating instructional videos, user manuals, or offering live training sessions to address employee questions and concerns. Additionally, ongoing technical support should be made available to ensure employees can overcome any challenges they encounter while using the new technology.

Integrating emerging technologies such as VR, AR, and AI-driven learning platforms into learning programs can significantly enhance the overall learning experience for employees. L&D professionals must carefully assess the suitability of new technologies, pilot and evaluate their effectiveness, and provide training and support for employees using these tools. By staying informed about the latest technological advancements and incorporating them into their learning programs, L&D professionals can ensure their organization remains at the forefront of innovation, providing employees with the most effective and engaging learning experiences possible.

4.4 LEARNING AGILITY - MEASURING THE IMPACT OF LEARNING PROGRAMS

To demonstrate the value of learning programs and continuously improve their effectiveness, L&D professionals must develop robust methods for measuring their impact. This chapter provides a practical, step-by-step guide to measuring the impact of learning programs, focusing on key performance indicators (KPIs), data collection and analysis methods, and strategies for communicating results to organizational leaders and stakeholders.

STEP 1: DEFINE KEY PERFORMANCE INDICATORS (KPIS)

Identify the most relevant KPIs for your learning programs, which may include:

Learning outcomes: Measure the extent to which employees have acquired new knowledge, skills, or abilities. Example KPI: Increase in average test scores following a training program.

Employee engagement: Assess how actively and enthusiastically employees participate in learning programs. Example KPI: Course completion rates or average time spent on learning activities.

Behavior change: Evaluate whether employees apply new skills and knowledge in their day-to-day work. Example KPI: Increase in the adoption of a specific process or tool after completing a training program.

STEP 2: COLLECT AND ANALYZE DATA

Implement methods for collecting and analyzing data on learning program effectiveness:

Learning analytics: Use learning management system (LMS) data to track employee progress, engagement, and performance. Example: Monitor employee progress through an online course and identify areas where they may need additional support. See chapter 4.5 for more on Learning analytics.

Feedback surveys: Collect employee feedback on learning programs through post-training surveys, focus groups, or one-on-one interviews. Example: Conduct a survey to assess employee satisfaction with the training program and gather suggestions for improvement.

STEP 3: COMMUNICATE THE IMPACT OF LEARNING PROGRAMS

Develop strategies for communicating the impact of learning programs to organizational leaders and stakeholders:

Create a comprehensive impact report: Compile data from various sources (LMS data, feedback surveys, performance metrics) to create a holistic view of the learning program's impact. Include visuals, such as charts and graphs, to make the data more accessible and engaging.

Share success stories: Highlight specific examples of how the learning program has led to positive outcomes for individuals, teams, or the organization as a whole. Example: Share a case study of an employee who successfully applied new skills from a training program to improve their job performance.

Regularly update stakeholders: Keep organizational leaders and stakeholders informed about the progress and impact of learning programs through periodic updates, meetings, or presentations.

By following these practical steps and focusing on measurable KPIs, L&D professionals can design future-ready learning programs that not only address the changing skill requirements of the workforce but also foster a culture of continuous learning and innovation within their organizations. This data-driven approach enables L&D professionals to demonstrate the value of their initiatives and secure ongoing support and resources for their learning and development efforts.

CHAPTER 5: ADAPTING LEARNING PROGRAMS TO REMOTE AND HYBRID WORK ENVIRONMENTS

5.1 THE SHIFT TO REMOTE AND HYBRID WORK MODELS

As discussed in chapter 1.5, the rapid transition to remote work during the global pandemic has reshaped the way organizations operate. As businesses adapt to this new reality, many are adopting hybrid work models, where employees split their time between working remotely and working in a physical office. This shift has significant implications for learning and development, as L&D professionals must now create learning programs that cater to employees in a variety of work environments, taking into account the unique challenges and opportunities posed by remote and hybrid work arrangements.

Survey your workforce to understand their preferences and needs for remote and hybrid work arrangements. Regularly review and update company policies to accommodate remote and hybrid workers. Encourage open communication and feedback from employees to identify and address any challenges in the remote and hybrid work environment.

5.2 DESIGNING LEARNING PROGRAMS FOR REMOTE AND HYBRID TEAMS

Creating effective learning programs for remote and hybrid teams requires a thoughtful approach to instructional design that considers the unique challenges and opportunities these work environments present. In this chapter, we outline strategies for designing learning programs tailored to remote and hybrid teams, focusing on asynchronous and synchronous learning methods, collaborative learning experiences, and ensuring accessibility for all employees.

5.2.1 ASYNCHRONOUS AND SYNCHRONOUS LEARNING METHODS

Balancing self-paced (asynchronous) and instructor-led (synchronous) training is critical for accommodating employees in different time zones and with varying schedules. Asynchronous learning methods, such as pre-recorded video lessons, e-learning modules, and self-guided resources, enable employees to learn at their own pace and on their own time. Synchronous learning methods, including live webinars and virtual workshops, facilitate real-time interaction and collaboration among team members. Combining both approaches in your learning programs ensures flexibility and inclusivity for all employees.

5.2.2 COLLABORATIVE LEARNING EXPERIENCES

Remote and hybrid work environments can lead to feelings of isolation and disconnection among team members. Integrating collaborative learning experiences into your learning programs can help foster a sense of community and promote knowledge sharing. Tools such as virtual whiteboards, like Miro, breakout rooms, and online discussion forums can facilitate collaboration and enable employees to learn from each other's experiences and perspectives.

5.2.3 ENSURING ACCESSIBILITY

Designing learning programs that are accessible to all employees, regardless of location, language, or disability, is essential for inclusivity and effectiveness. Ensure that your learning materials are available in multiple formats (e.g., video, text, audio) and languages, and consider incorporating closed captions, transcripts, and screen reader compatibility for employees with disabilities. Additionally, provide clear instructions for accessing and navigating learning resources and offer technical support to address any barriers employees may encounter.

To ensure accessibility in your learning programs:

Review your existing learning materials and identify areas where accessibility improvements can be made, such as adding captions to videos, providing transcripts for audio content, or ensuring text is screen reader-friendly.

Consult with accessibility experts and employees with disabilities to gain insights into their needs and preferences, and use this feedback to guide the development of accessible learning content.

Train facilitators and instructors on best practices for inclusive learning environments, such as using clear language, providing alternative formats for content, and being mindful of diverse learning needs during live sessions.

5.3 OVERCOMING CHALLENGES IN REMOTE AND HYBRID LEARNING

5.3.1 BUILDING AND MAINTAINING ENGAGEMENT

Keeping remote and hybrid employees engaged and motivated in their learning journeys can be challenging, but it is essential for the success of your learning programs. By incorporating interactive elements, regularly soliciting feedback, and recognizing learning achievements, you can foster a more engaging and motivating learning experience for your employees.

Embrace interactivity: The use of interactive elements in your learning programs helps to create a dynamic and engaging experience for employees. Incorporating quizzes, polls, and gamification not only helps to assess comprehension but also encourages active participation and friendly competition. As the renowned educator and author, Edgar Dale, once said, **"We learn by doing, and real engagement comes from the active involvement of the learner."**

Cultivate a feedback culture: Regularly soliciting employee feedback demonstrates your commitment to continuous improvement and allows you to identify areas for enhancement in your learning programs. As Bill Gates famously said, "We all need people who will give us feedback. That's how we improve." Encourage employees to provide honest, constructive feedback and be open to making adjustments based on their input.

Set clear goals and expectations: Establishing clear learning goals and expectations helps employees understand the purpose and desired outcomes of your learning programs. As management consultant Peter Drucker once noted, "You can't manage what you can't measure." By setting measurable goals, employees can track their progress and stay motivated throughout their learning journey.

Recognize and celebrate achievements: Recognizing and celebrating employees' learning achievements reinforces motivation and demonstrates the value your organization places on continuous learning. According to leadership expert Ken Blanchard, *"Feedback is the breakfast of champions."* By acknowledging employees' accomplishments, you inspire them to continue learning and growing.

Foster a sense of community: Encourage employees to share their learning experiences and insights with their peers, creating a learning community where everyone can learn from one another. As the saying goes, *"Alone we can do so little; together we can do so much."* By fostering a sense of community, employees can support one another, exchange ideas, and build camaraderie, further enhancing their engagement and motivation in the learning process.

5.3.2 SUPPORTING EMPLOYEE WELL-BEING

The stressors associated with remote and hybrid work environments can significantly impact employee mental health and well-being. It is crucial for L&D professionals to adopt a holistic approach to employee well-being, incorporating well-being-focused learning initiatives, resources, and support from organizational leaders.

Mental fitness: Repositioning mental health as mental fitness emphasizes the importance of proactive mental well-being strategies and encourages employees to build their mental resilience. Just as physical fitness involves regular exercise and a healthy lifestyle, mental fitness requires ongoing efforts to maintain and improve mental health, such as stress management, mindfulness, and self-reflection.

Well-being-focused learning initiatives: Incorporate well-being-focused learning initiatives and resources into your programs, such as stress management workshops, mindfulness training, and mental health support resources. These initiatives help employees develop coping strategies, enhance emotional intelligence, and build resilience in the face of work-related stressors.

Leadership impact: Encourage managers to actively support their team members' well-being and model healthy work habits. Leaders play a crucial role in shaping the mental health environment within their teams. As the saying goes, *"People don't leave jobs; they leave managers."* Effective leaders prioritize employee well-being, promote work-life balance, and create psychologically safe spaces for their teams to thrive.

AQme assessment: The AQme assessment is a valuable tool that provides insights into work-stress, team and company support, and the emotional health of the workplace. By identifying employees at risk of burnout and measuring their adaptability, organizations can implement targeted interventions to support their well-being and foster a healthier work environment. This early detection is essential for retaining happy, engaged, and highly innovative teams.

The adaptability advantage: Understanding and addressing employees' well-being is crucial for maintaining a workforce that can adapt and innovate in the face of rapid change. Employees who feel supported and have access to the necessary resources to manage their mental health are more likely to be engaged, productive, and creative. By fostering a culture that prioritizes well-being, organizations can build and maintain high-performing teams that are better equipped to navigate the challenges of the modern work environment.

5.3.3 MAINTAINING A STRONG LEARNING COMMUNITY

B uilding and maintaining a strong learning community is essential for supporting remote and hybrid team members' learning and development. By fostering connections, a sense of belonging, and opportunities for informal learning, L&D professionals can create an environment where employees thrive and continuously grow.

Online platforms for connection: Establish online platforms for employees to connect, share ideas, and ask questions. Virtual water cooler chats, learning-focused discussion forums, and social media groups can facilitate communication, encourage knowledge-sharing, and build camaraderie among team members. These platforms create a sense of belonging, regardless of employees' physical locations.

Virtual team-building events: Organize regular virtual team-building events that promote interaction and collaboration among team members. Activities such as virtual escape rooms, trivia nights, or online workshops can help break down barriers, foster a sense of unity, and make remote employees feel more connected to their colleagues.

Cross-functional collaboration: Encourage cross-functional collaboration to strengthen relationships among team members and create opportunities for informal learning. By working together on projects or participating in cross-departmental initiatives, employees can gain exposure to different perspectives, expand their skill sets, and develop a broader understanding of the organization's goals and objectives.

Mentorship and peer coaching: Implement mentorship and peer coaching programs to promote ongoing learning and development. Pairing employees with more experienced colleagues or peers with complementary skill sets can facilitate knowledge transfer, provide support, and encourage continuous growth. This also helps build strong connections and trust within the organization.

Celebrating successes and learning milestones: Acknowledge and celebrate employees' learning achievements and milestones. By recognizing their accomplishments, you reinforce the importance of continuous learning and development. Sharing success stories can inspire other employees, create a sense of pride within the community, and motivate team members to strive for their own learning goals.

CHAPTER 6: LEVERAGING TECHNOLOGY TO ENHANCE LEARNING AND DEVELOPMENT

6.1 EMBRACING DIGITAL TRANSFORMATION IN LEARNING AND DEVELOPMENT

L&D professionals, by very definition, stand at the forefront of technological development and forward-leaps in knowledge, and are responsible for ensuring that employees remain sufficiently skilled and literate with developing paradigms and technologies in order for a business to thrive.

A significant portion of training employees in today's age undergo will involve software fluency and adapting to a rapidly changing environment. It is therefore essential to "practice what you preach" and embrace digital transformation and integrate technology into learning programs to create engaging, effective, and accessible experiences for employees. This chapter will explore various technologies that can be utilized to enhance learning and development in the modern workplace.

LEARNING MANAGEMENT SYSTEMS (LMS)

LMSs are centralized platforms for managing, delivering, and tracking learning activities. They enable organizations to efficiently administer training programs, monitor employee progress, and assess learning outcomes. Key features of an LMS include course management, assessment tools, reporting and analytics, and integration with HR systems.

LEARNING EXPERIENCE PLATFORMS (LXP)

LXPs are next-generation learning platforms designed to deliver personalized, engaging, and social learning experiences. They combine the functionality of an LMS with advanced features like content curation, artificial intelligence-driven recommendations, and social learning tools. LXPs enable employees to take control of their learning journeys, discover and share relevant content, and collaborate with their peers.

VIRTUAL AND AUGMENTED REALITY (VR/AR)

Virtual and augmented reality technologies offer immersive and interactive learning experiences that can significantly enhance employee engagement and retention. VR simulations can replicate real-world scenarios, allowing employees to practice and develop skills in a safe and controlled environment. AR can overlay digital information onto the physical world, providing contextual guidance and support during on-the-job training.

6.2 HARNESSING THE POWER OF ARTIFICIAL INTELLIGENCE AND CHATBOTS

6.2.1 AI-DRIVEN PERSONALIZATION

A rtificial Intelligence (AI) has the potential to revolutionize the way L&D professionals approach learning and development by offering highly personalized learning experiences for each employee. AI-driven personalization leverages machine learning algorithms to analyze employee data, such as learning history, performance metrics, and skill levels. This information enables the creation of tailored learning experiences that target individual needs, preferences, and knowledge gaps.

For example, AI-driven platforms can recommend specific learning resources or courses based on an employee's role, past performance, and identify areas for improvement. These recommendations ensure that employees receive the most relevant and impactful learning experiences, which can lead to better skill development and improved job performance.

Furthermore, AI can adjust learning paths in real-time based on an employee's progress, ensuring that they are continually challenged and engaged. This adaptive learning approach keeps the content fresh and relevant, promoting sustained engagement and facilitating long-term knowledge retention.

Chatbots, powered by AI and natural language processing, can play a significant role in enhancing learning experiences for employees. These virtual assistants can be integrated into learning platforms and serve as a resource for answering questions, providing guidance, and offering real-time support to learners.

One practical application of chatbots in learning and development is providing instant feedback on employee performance. For example, during a training exercise or assessment, a chatbot can analyze an employee's response, compare it to the correct answer, and offer immediate feedback or clarification. This immediate feedback can help employees better understand and internalize the concepts they are learning.

Chatbots can also facilitate on-demand learning by providing instant access to relevant information and resources. Employees can interact with chatbots through text or voice commands, asking questions or requesting information related to their learning objectives. By offering personalized, just-in-time support, chatbots can enhance the overall learning experience and promote knowledge retention.

AI-driven personalization and chatbots can significantly enhance learning experiences by offering tailored content, real-time support, and adaptive learning paths. By harnessing the power of AI, L&D professionals can create more engaging and effective learning programs that cater to the unique needs of each employee.

6.2.2 THE IMPACT OF CHATGPT-4

Advanced AI models leveraging large language models (LLM) like ChatGPT-4, will become valuable tools for L&D professionals, offering versatile support for learning and development. By harnessing the power of these gernerative AI tools, organizations can create more dynamic, engaging, and effective learning experiences.

Real-Time Assistance: One of the most significant benefits of chatbots like ChatGPT-4 is their ability to provide real-time assistance to learners. They can quickly answer questions, offer guidance, and clarify concepts, making it easier for employees to access the information they need when they need it. This on-demand support enables learners to overcome challenges, improve their understanding, and maintain their momentum during the learning process.

Interactive Learning Experiences: Chatbots can be used to create interactive learning experiences that foster employee engagement and facilitate knowledge retention. They can simulate conversations with learners, allowing them to practice their communication skills, apply new concepts, and receive instant feedback. This interactive approach encourages employees to actively participate in their learning and helps them internalize new information more effectively.

Contextual Learning: By simulating real-life situations and conversations, chatbots like ChatGPT-4 can help employees apply their knowledge in context. This contextual learning approach enables employees to better understand how their new skills and knowledge can be applied in the workplace, improving their ability to transfer learning to job performance.

Mentoring and Coaching: ChatGPT-4 and other advanced chatbots can serve as virtual mentors or coaches, offering personalized support and guidance throughout the learning journey. They can help employees set learning goals, track their progress, and offer encouragement and motivation along the way. This tailored support can significantly enhance the overall learning experience, promoting employee development and growth.

Chatbots like ChatGPT-4 can be powerful allies in learning and development efforts, offering real-time assistance, interactive learning experiences, contextual learning, and personalized mentoring. By incorporating these advanced AI models into their learning programs, L&D professionals can create more engaging and effective learning experiences that cater to employees' unique needs and preferences.

6.3 LEARNING ANALYTICS

Learning analytics is a powerful tool for L&D professionals, as it enables them to make informed decisions about their learning programs based on data. By collecting, analyzing, and interpreting data related to employee learning, they can optimize learning experiences and align them with business objectives. This chapter will discuss the various aspects of learning analytics and its benefits.

6.3.1 DATA COLLECTION AND TRACKING

Effective learning analytics begins with collecting relevant data. L&D professionals can gather data from various sources, such as learning management systems (LMS), e-learning platforms, and feedback surveys. Key data points to track may include employee engagement, progress, performance, and assessment scores. This data can provide valuable insights into the learning process and help identify areas for improvement.

6.3.2 DATA ANALYSIS AND INTERPRETATION

Once data has been collected, it must be analyzed and interpreted to gain actionable insights. L&D

professionals can use various analytical techniques, including descriptive, diagnostic, predictive, and prescriptive analytics, to better understand the current state of their learning programs, diagnose issues, forecast future performance, and make recommendations for improvement.

6.3.3 CONTINUOUS IMPROVEMENT AND OPTIMIZATION

Learning analytics allows L&D professionals to continuously improve and optimize their learning programs by making data-driven adjustments. By identifying trends and patterns in employee learning, they can refine their instructional design, delivery methods, and learning content to better meet employee needs and preferences. This iterative approach ensures that learning programs remain relevant, engaging, and effective over time.

6.3.4 ALIGNING LEARNING OUTCOMES WITH BUSINESS OBJECTIVES

One of the primary goals of learning analytics is to help organizations align their learning programs with their overall business objectives. By analyzing the relationship between learning outcomes and key performance indicators (KPIs), L&D professionals can ensure that their programs are contributing to organizational success and growth. This alignment can help demonstrate the value of L&D initiatives to stakeholders and secure ongoing support and investment.

6.3.5 DEMONSTRATING THE IMPACT OF L&D ON OVERALL PERFORMANCE

Learning analytics can also be used to showcase the impact of L&D initiatives on overall organizational performance. By correlating learning outcomes with metrics such as employee productivity, retention, and customer satisfaction, L&D professionals can build a compelling case for the value of their programs. This evidence can help secure buy-in from senior leaders, promote a culture of continuous learning, and ultimately drive organizational success.

Learning analytics plays a crucial role in modern L&D practices. By collecting, analyzing, and interpreting data, L&D professionals can optimize their learning programs, align them with business objectives, and demonstrate their impact on overall performance. Embracing learning analytics can significantly enhance the effectiveness and value of L&D initiatives within an organization. See more ideas in chapter **Chapter 7: Measuring the Impact of L&D Initiatives**

6.4 BUILDING A FUTURE-PROOF L&D STRATEGY

It is crucial to develop a future-proof strategy that can evolve alongside your organization's needs and the dynamic shifts within the industry. This chapter will discuss key components of building a future-proof L&D strategy, focusing on staying informed and adapting to new trends, fostering a culture of innovation and experimentation, and collaborating with cross-functional teams and external partners.

By adopting a proactive approach to learning and development, you can ensure that your organization is well-equipped to navigate the challenges of an increasingly complex and unpredictable world. This requires a combination of staying current with emerging trends, embracing innovation, and fostering strong connections with others in your field. By incorporating these principles into your L&D strategy, you can create a robust foundation for continuous improvement and organizational success.

6.4.1 STAYING INFORMED AND ADAPTING TO NEW TRENDS

To build a future-proof L&D strategy, it is essential to stay informed about emerging trends, technologies, and best practices in the L&D field. By being aware of the latest developments, you can anticipate the needs of your organization and its employees, and incorporate innovative solutions into your learning programs.

To stay informed, consider the following approaches:

Subscribe to industry publications and blogs: Follow reputable sources of information, such as journals, magazines, and blogs that focus on L&D and related fields. These resources can provide valuable insights into current trends, case studies, and expert opinions.

→   *THE ELEARNING INDUSTRY BLOG*

→   *TRAINING JOURNAL*

→   *CHIEF LEARNING OFFICER MAGAZINE*

→   *THE ASSOCIATION FOR TALENT DEVELOPMENT (ATD) BLOG*

Participate in conferences and webinars: Attend industry conferences, webinars, and workshops to hear from leading experts, share ideas, and network with other L&D professionals. These events can offer invaluable opportunities for learning and staying up-to-date on the latest innovations.

→ **ATD INTERNATIONAL CONFERENCE & EXPOSITION**

→ **LEARNING TECHNOLOGIES CONFERENCE**

→ **DEVLEARN CONFERENCE & EXPO**

→ **ELEARNING GUILD WEBINARS**

Engage with professional networks: Join professional associations, online communities, and social media groups related to L&D. These networks can facilitate the exchange of ideas, best practices, and real-world experiences among L&D professionals.

→ **ASSOCIATION FOR TALENT DEVELOPMENT (ATD)**

→ **INTERNATIONAL SOCIETY FOR TECHNOLOGY IN EDUCATION (ISTE)**

→ **L&D CONNECT (*LINKEDIN GROUP*)**

→ **LEARNING AND DEVELOPMENT (L&D) DISCUSSION GROUP (*LINKEDIN GROUP*)**

Collaborate with colleagues: Foster open communication and knowledge sharing within your L&D team and your organization as a whole. Encourage team members to share insights and resources they have encountered in their own learning journeys.

→ HOLD REGULAR TEAM MEETINGS TO SHARE
   INSIGHTS AND RESOURCES

→ CREATE AN INTERNAL KNOWLEDGE-SHARING
   PLATFORM OR DISCUSSION FORUM

→ ORGANIZE "LUNCH AND LEARN" SESSIONS WHERE
   TEAM MEMBERS PRESENT ON A TOPIC OF INTEREST

→ ENCOURAGE CROSS-FUNCTIONAL COLLABORATION
   AND LEARNING EXCHANGES BETWEEN
   DEPARTMENTS

Monitor advancements in related fields: Keep an eye on developments in fields like technology, psychology, and neuroscience, as breakthroughs in these areas can have significant implications for L&D.

→ READ ARTICLES AND REPORTS FROM TECHNOLOGY-
   FOCUSED SOURCES LIKE TECHCRUNCH OR WIRED

→ FOLLOW RESEARCH PUBLICATIONS IN PSYCHOLOGY,
   SUCH AS THE JOURNAL OF APPLIED PSYCHOLOGY
   OR PSYCHOLOGICAL SCIENCE

→ KEEP UP WITH ADVANCEMENTS IN
   NEUROSCIENCE BY READING JOURNALS LIKE
   NATURE NEUROSCIENCE OR THE JOURNAL OF
   NEUROSCIENCE

→ ATTEND INTERDISCIPLINARY CONFERENCES AND
   EVENTS, SUCH AS THE SOCIETY FOR NEUROSCIENCE

ANNUAL MEETING OR THE INTERNATIONAL CONFERENCE ON LEARNING AND MEMORY

Continuously adapting your strategies and approaches in response to new trends and insights will enable you to remain relevant and effective in the face of change. By being proactive and committed to lifelong learning, you can ensure that your L&D strategy is well-aligned with the evolving needs of your organization and its workforce.

6.4.2 FOSTERING A CULTURE OF INNOVATION AND EXPERIMENTATION

Cultivating a culture of innovation and experimentation within your L&D team is crucial for staying ahead of industry trends and continuously improving the effectiveness of your learning programs. By promoting curiosity and a willingness to explore new ideas, tools, and methodologies, you can drive continuous learning and growth within your team and the broader organization.

To foster a culture of innovation and experimentation:

Encourage open communication: Create a safe space where team members feel comfortable sharing their ideas, suggestions, and concerns. Encourage honest feedback and open discussions about potential improvements and innovations in your learning programs.

Allocate resources for exploration: Set aside time and resources for team members to explore new tools, technologies, and learning methodologies. This could include attending workshops or conferences, engaging in self-directed learning, or experimenting with new tools during designated "innovation days."

Implement a continuous improvement mindset: Regularly review your learning programs and initiatives to identify areas for improvement or potential innovations. Engage your team in the process of continuous improvement by involving them in the evaluation of learning programs and soliciting their ideas for enhancements.

Foster cross-functional collaboration: Encourage collaboration between your L&D team and other departments within your organization. Cross-functional collaboration can spark new ideas, provide fresh perspectives, and help identify emerging trends and opportunities for innovation.

One useful approach to foster this culture is to apply the **3 Horizons Framework.** The 3 Horizons Framework is a strategic model that helps organizations plan for the future by dividing their innovation efforts into three distinct horizons, each with its own focus and goals:

Horizon 1: Core innovations - These are focused on enhancing and maintaining the organization's existing learning programs, tools, and processes. In the context of L&D, this could involve refining current course content, optimizing delivery methods, and improving the user experience. To foster innovation in Horizon 1, encourage your team to identify and implement incremental improvements to existing programs.

Horizon 2: Adjacent innovations - These involve expanding the organization's capabilities into new but related areas. In L&D, this could include exploring new learning technologies, such as virtual reality or AI-driven platforms, or developing programs that address emerging skill needs within the organization. Encourage your team to collaborate with other departments and stay informed about industry trends to identify potential adjacent innovations.

Horizon 3: Disruptive innovations - These are long-term, transformative innovations that have the potential to redefine the organization's approach to learning and development. Examples might include implementing a completely new learning model or leveraging cutting-edge technology to revolutionize the learning experience. To foster innovation in

Horizon 3, create a culture that encourages experimentation, tolerates failure, and supports long-term, high-risk projects.

In the context of the 3 Horizons Framework, **organizational ambidexterity** is essential for achieving success across all three horizons. Ambidexterity refers to an organization's ability to simultaneously exploit existing capabilities (Horizon 1) while exploring new opportunities for growth (Horizons 2 and 3). This balance enables the organization to maintain its core strengths while also staying agile and responsive to emerging trends and disruptive innovations.

As the world becomes increasingly interconnected and technology continues to advance at an exponential rate, the timelines for each horizon have significantly compressed. Disruptive innovations and transformations that once took decades to unfold now occur within years or even months. Consequently, organizations need to be agile and prepared to adapt their L&D strategies at a faster pace to remain competitive and relevant in this rapidly changing environment.

To navigate this accelerated landscape, L&D professionals must closely monitor industry trends, embrace a culture of continuous learning, and actively collaborate with cross-functional teams to identify and capitalize on new opportunities. Encouraging organizational ambidexterity ensures that your

L&D team remains adept at managing both the core and the cutting-edge aspects of learning and development, ultimately creating a future-proof and resilient L&D strategy that thrives in our exponential world.

By applying the 3 Horizons Framework within your L&D team, you can strategically allocate resources and efforts across different types of innovations, ensuring a balanced approach that maintains current strengths while also exploring new opportunities for growth and improvement.

6.4.3 COLLABORATING WITH CROSS-FUNCTIONAL TEAMS & PARTNERS

Collaborate with cross-functional teams within your organization and engage external partners to stay current with industry trends and best practices. Leverage the expertise and insights of others to continually enhance your L&D programs and strategies.

Leveraging technology and innovations is essential for experienced L&D professionals seeking to remain at the forefront of their field. By embracing digital transformation, implementing learning technologies, and harnessing the power of artificial intelligence, you can deliver engaging, relevant, and impactful learning experiences that drive lasting success for your organization. Furthermore, fostering a future-proof L&D strategy by staying informed, encouraging innovation, and collaborating with others ensures your organization remains agile and responsive in an ever-changing landscape.

CHAPTER 7: ALTERNATIVE STRATEGIES FOR EXPERIMENTAL L&D PROFESSIONALS

As a highly experienced L&D professional, your expertise and deep understanding of learning strategies enables you to design programs that have a significant and lasting impact on your organization. This entails aligning learning initiatives with business objectives, creating learner-centered experiences, and measuring the effectiveness of your programs. By focusing on these key areas, you can ensure that your learning and development efforts not only support individual growth but also contribute to the overall success of your organization. In this chapter, we will explore various approaches and best practices for designing high-impact learning programs that drive meaningful results.

Drawing Inspiration from Diverse Cultures and Historical Examples. To enhance their L&D strategies, experienced professionals can draw inspiration from diverse cultures and historical examples. Exploring these approaches can provide fresh perspectives and novel ideas to incorporate into modern learning programs.

7.1.1 The Socratic Method (Ancient Greece)

The Socratic Method, attributed to the Greek philosopher Socrates, is a form of dialogue-based learning where participants engage in a series of probing questions and answers to stimulate critical thinking and illuminate ideas. By incorporating the Socratic Method into learning programs, L&D professionals can foster deeper understanding and reflection among learners.

7.1.2 Shuhari (Japan)

Shuhari is a Japanese concept that outlines the stages of learning mastery: Shu (obeying and learning fundamentals), Ha (detaching from and refining the teachings), and Ri (transcending the teachings and creating one's own path). L&D professionals can use this framework to guide employees through different stages of skill development and encourage them to eventually become independent problem-solvers and innovators.

7.1.3 Apprenticeship Model (Medieval Europe)

In Medieval Europe, the apprenticeship model was widely used to develop skilled craftsmen. Apprentices learned from experienced masters, who provided hands-on training and mentorship over an extended period. Modern L&D professionals can adapt this model by incorporating mentorship, on-the-job training, and long-term skill development into their learning programs.

7.1.4 Ubuntu Philosophy (Southern Africa)

The Ubuntu philosophy, originating from Southern Africa, emphasizes the interconnectedness of people and the importance of collaboration and community. By embracing the principles of Ubuntu in learning programs, L&D professionals can foster a culture of mutual support, knowledge sharing, and collective growth.

7.2 IMPLEMENTING LESS-KNOWN STRATEGIES IN YOUR L&D PROGRAMS

To incorporate these diverse cultural and historical strategies into your L&D programs, consider the following steps:

Research and explore: Investigate different cultures, historical periods, and educational philosophies to discover new approaches that could complement or enhance your current L&D initiatives.

Adapt and customize: Tailor the selected strategies to suit your organization's context, values, and learning objectives.

Pilot and evaluate: Test the adapted strategies in a small-scale pilot program, gather feedback from participants, and evaluate their effectiveness before implementing them on a larger scale.

Integrate and refine: Integrate the successful strategies into your existing L&D programs and continuously refine them based on feedback and evolving needs.

By drawing on diverse cultural and historical examples, highly experienced L&D professionals can enrich their learning programs, foster innovation, and drive continuous improvement in their organizations.

7.3 ALIGNING LEARNING WITH BUSINESS OBJECTIVES

Aligning learning initiatives with your organization's goals and priorities is crucial for ensuring that your L&D efforts have the desired impact. By understanding the strategic objectives of your organization, you can develop targeted learning programs that directly support these goals, drive performance improvements, and demonstrate the value of L&D. Here are a few strategies to get you started and help you align learning with business objectives:

Collaborate with key stakeholders: Work closely with leaders, managers, and other stakeholders to gain a deep understanding of your organization's strategic priorities and the skills needed to achieve them. This collaboration will enable you to develop learning programs that address critical skill gaps and support the achievement of business objectives.

Conduct skills gap analyses: Regularly assess your workforce's current capabilities and identify areas where new or improved skills are needed to achieve organizational goals. Use this information to design targeted learning initiatives that address these specific needs and contribute to the success of your organization.

Set clear, measurable learning outcomes: Establish specific, measurable learning outcomes that are directly linked to business objectives. By setting clear expectations and goals for your learning programs, you can more effectively measure their impact and demonstrate the ROI of your L&D initiatives.

Align learning content with organizational culture and values: Ensure that the content of your learning programs is consistent with your organization's culture and values. This alignment helps to reinforce the desired behaviors, attitudes, and mindsets that support your organization's strategic goals.

Monitor progress and adjust accordingly: Regularly review the progress of your learning initiatives against the established business objectives. Use this information to make any necessary adjustments to your programs, ensuring that they continue to effectively support the achievement of organizational goals.

7.3.1 CREATING LEARNER-CENTERED EXPERIENCES

Whilst it is important to align the learning content with organisational values, it is also important to balance this organization-centric perspective with learner-centered experiences; developing learner-centered experiences is vital for keeping employees engaged, motivated, and committed to their growth. By concentrating on the distinct needs and inclinations of your employees, you can create learning programs that truly connect with them and yield more impactful outcomes. Consider the following approaches for crafting learner-centered experiences:

Learning Styles: Recognize and cater to the diverse learning styles of your employees. Some individuals may prefer visual or auditory learning, while others might thrive with hands-on, experiential learning. Incorporate a variety of learning methods and resources to accommodate these diverse preferences and facilitate more effective knowledge retention.

Real-world Application: Ensure that your learning programs incorporate practical, real-world scenarios and challenges that employees can relate to. By providing opportunities for learners to apply their newly acquired skills and knowledge in real-life contexts, they will better understand the relevance of their learning and be more likely to retain and use the information in their daily work.

Empowering Learner Choices: Offer employees the autonomy to choose their learning paths and resources. By providing a diverse range of learning options, employees can select the ones that resonate with them the most, leading to greater engagement and motivation. Additionally, involving learners in the decision-making process fosters a sense of ownership and responsibility for their personal development.

7.4 BUILDING A LEARNING CULTURE

Creating a learning culture within your organization is a critical component of any successful L&D strategy. A thriving learning culture not only fosters continuous development but also improves employee engagement, innovation, and adaptability to change. By actively promoting and supporting learning, you can unlock the full potential of your workforce and drive organizational growth.

In this chapter, we will explore three key strategies to build a robust learning culture: encouraging ownership and accountability, promoting collaboration and knowledge sharing, and recognizing and celebrating learning achievements. By implementing these strategies, you will cultivate an environment where learning is not just a one-time event but an ongoing process that empowers employees and leads to sustained success.

7.4.1 ENCOURAGING OWNERSHIP AND ACCOUNTABILITY

To foster a learning culture where employees feel empowered to take charge of their development, it is crucial to draw upon the latest research in psychology and motivation. This involves implementing strategies that tap into employees' intrinsic motivation and create a sense of ownership over their learning journey.

Integrating goal hierarchy concepts into your learning strategy can further encourage ownership and accountability.

Goal hierarchy refers to the organization of goals in a nested structure, from higher-level, abstract goals to lower-level, specific goals. This structure helps employees see how their individual learning objectives align with broader team and organizational goals, promoting a sense of purpose and direction.

Incorporate the principles of **Self-Determination Theory (SDT)**, which posits that individuals are intrinsically motivated when their needs for autonomy, competence, and relatedness are met. By providing employees with the tools and resources they need to learn and develop, you support their need for competence. Furthermore, giving them the freedom to choose their learning paths and set personal goals caters to their need for autonomy. Finally, fostering a sense of belonging and connectedness within the team or organization addresses their need for relatedness.

Support employees in setting and achieving their learning goals by helping them break down higher-level goals into smaller, more manageable sub-goals. This process can facilitate progress and build momentum, as employees can experience a sense of accomplishment as they work towards their larger objectives.

Encourage employees to adopt a growth mindset by emphasizing the importance of effort, continuous improvement, and learning from challenges, as outlined in Carol Dweck's growth mindset theory. Reinforce the idea that skills and abilities can be developed through hard work and persistence, rather than being fixed traits. In addition using elements from Angela Duckworth's research on grit, which is a combination of passion and perseverance, can help employees develop a sense of ownership and determination by encouraging them to identify their long-term goals and providing them with the necessary resources and support.

Finally, recognize and reward employees for their learning efforts and achievements through formal recognition programs, performance appraisals, or simple gestures like verbal praise or acknowledgement in team meetings. By celebrating their progress and accomplishments, you reinforce the importance of continuous learning and development while also fostering a culture of accountability.

By leveraging insights from research in psychology and motivation, and integrating goal hierarchy concepts, you can create an environment where employees feel empowered to take charge of their learning and development. Addressing their needs for autonomy, competence, and relatedness, by fostering a growth mindset, promoting grit, and aligning individual goals with broader organizational objectives will encourage a culture of ownership and accountability that drives lasting success.

7.4.2 PROMOTING COLLABORATION AND KNOWLEDGE SHARING

Fostering a culture of collaboration and knowledge sharing is essential for creating an environment where employees can learn from one another and contribute to collective growth. By incorporating the latest research and key psychological concepts into your L&D methodologies, you can promote effective collaboration and knowledge sharing that drives employee engagement and performance.

Social Learning Theory: According to Albert Bandura's Social Learning Theory, individuals learn by observing and imitating the behaviors of others. To promote social learning, create opportunities for employees to engage in collaborative activities, such as group projects, workshops, and team-based challenges. Encourage employees to share their expertise and insights through presentations, demonstrations, and informal discussions.

Communities of Practice: Research by Etienne Wenger and Jean Lave suggests that learning occurs in social contexts through participation in communities of practice, which are groups of individuals who share a common interest and collaborate to develop their skills and knowledge. Think of the old concept of a "guild": communities of individuals who share a particular profession or skill, and therefore form a group to pool resources and knowledge. Establish communities of practice within your organization by creating forums, discussion groups, and other platforms where employees can come together to share ideas, ask questions, and learn from one another.

Psychological Safety: is such a big topic - *(one for a whole new book)!*

The role of psychological safety in fostering collaboration and learning cannot be overstated. In a psychologically safe environment, individuals are comfortable expressing their ideas, voicing concerns, admitting mistakes, and asking questions without fear of judgment or punishment. Here's how you, as an L&D professional, can take concrete steps to promote psychological safety:

Step 1 Leadership Workshops: Run workshops for leaders and managers emphasizing the importance of psychological safety. Highlight its impact on team performance, innovation, and learning. Utilize real-life case studies and role-playing activities to make these workshops interactive and engaging.

Equip leaders with strategies to foster psychological safety, such as showing vulnerability, encouraging open communication, and responding positively to failures.

Step 2 Team Centric Development: Implement team-development activities that foster trust and mutual respect among team members. This could include collaborative problem-solving exercises or team retreats focusing on open communication. These activities can help create a sense of camaraderie, reducing the fear of judgment or punishment.

Step 3 FeedForward Culture: Next level 360's - Promote a culture of feedforward, where real-time insights and guidance are provided to drive immediate actions and future decisions. Unlike traditional feedback, which often focuses on past performance, feedforward is forward-thinking and action-oriented, providing individuals with actionable steps they can take within the next 48 hours. To implement this, encourage leaders and team members to share observations and suggestions during daily interactions, meetings, or after significant events. Stress the importance of quick implementation, emphasizing actions that can be taken immediately to enhance performance. This in-the-moment advice can be more productive and impactful, fostering an environment of continuous growth and adaptation.

Step 4 Learning from Failure: Normalize failures as opportunities for learning rather than occasions for punishment. Share stories of successful people who experienced failure, conduct 'failure forums' where employees discuss mistakes and what they learned from them, or even reward the 'best' failure of the month. This practice sends a clear message that taking risks and making mistakes is an accepted part of growth and innovation.

Step 5 Monitoring Psychological Safety: Consider running regular surveys, or deeper scientific assessments like our AQme profile. Alongside discussions to assess the level of psychological safety within teams. Address any concerns raised promptly and effectively. Incorporating psychological safety metrics into broader performance assessments can also emphasize its importance within the organization. As mentioned the scientific measurement of psychological safety is a dimension in our AQ model. Plus we have developed training and resources to help specifically enhance this. A multiplier can be achieved by leveraging our AQ Certified Partner Network.

Reciprocity: Robert Cialdini's research on the psychology of persuasion suggests that people are more likely to engage in collaborative behaviors when they feel a sense of reciprocity. To promote knowledge sharing, create a culture where employees are encouraged to help one another and feel comfortable asking for assistance. Recognize and reward individuals who actively contribute to the learning of their peers.

Motivation: Self-Determination Theory (SDT), describes the need for autonomy, competence, and relatedness to increase intrinsic motivation for collaboration and knowledge sharing. Ensure that employees understand the value of working together and are provided with the necessary tools, resources, and support to effectively collaborate.

Network Building: Encourage employees to build strong professional networks both within and outside the organization. Strong networks facilitate the exchange of information and ideas, leading to increased knowledge sharing and learning. Offer opportunities for employees to attend industry conferences, participate in professional associations, and engage with external partners.

By integrating these research-based concepts and strategies, you can promote a culture of collaboration and knowledge sharing within your organization, ultimately driving employee engagement, learning, and performance.

How The Social Learning Theory applies to L&D to enhance learning experiences and promote adaptability intelligence:

As mentioned earlier, Albert Bandura's Social Learning Theory is a psychological framework that emphasizes the importance of observational learning in shaping human behavior. According to Bandura, people learn not only through their own direct experiences but also by observing and imitating the actions of others. This theory has significant implications for learning and development (L&D) professionals, as it highlights the role of social interactions in the learning process, and it can be closely tied to the concept of adaptability intelligence. In fact, Albert Bandura's Social Learning Theory further underpins the development of adaptability intelligence (AQ). The essence of AQ is the ability to change behavior and strategies in response to evolving circumstances. According to Bandura's theory, individuals learn new behaviors and modify existing ones by observing others, especially those seen as role models. This observational learning process is pivotal to adaptability; seeing how others respond to change allows individuals to adopt successful strategies and discard ineffective ones without undergoing the trial-and-error process themselves. Thus, Bandura's theory informs the creation of learning environments where adaptability is not just taught but also observed, modeled, and practiced. In the rapidly changing corporate landscape, L&D professionals can leverage this powerful link to foster high AQ teams, driving organizational resilience and success.

Attention: For observational learning to occur, individuals must pay attention to the behavior being modeled. L&D professionals can capture the attention of learners by using engaging content, such as videos, animations, and real-life examples, as well as by emphasizing the relevance of the material to the learner's job or personal interests.

Retention: Learners must be able to remember the observed behavior to reproduce it later. L&D professionals can facilitate retention by incorporating repetition, practice, and reinforcement into learning activities. They can also use techniques such as storytelling, mnemonic devices, and visual aids to enhance memory.

Reproduction: Learners must possess the necessary skills and abilities to reproduce the observed behavior. L&D professionals can support learners in developing these skills by providing step-by-step guidance, demonstrations, and opportunities for practice. Feedback and coaching can also be used to help learners refine their skills and achieve mastery.

Learners must be motivated to imitate the observed behavior. L&D professionals can enhance motivation by creating a supportive learning environment where employees feel valued, respected, and encouraged to take risks. They can also use incentives, such as recognition, rewards, and career advancement opportunities, to motivate learners to engage in the desired behaviors.

Applying the Social Learning Theory to improve adaptability intelligence (AQ) involves creating opportunities for employees to observe and learn from the adaptive behaviors of others. L&D professionals can:

Showcase best practices and success stories from employees who have demonstrated adaptability in their roles. This can be done through case studies, videos, or panel discussions.

Encourage peer-to-peer learning and mentoring, where employees can learn from the experiences and expertise of their colleagues, particularly those who excel in adaptability. Plus, **incorporate role modeling, simulations**, and group exercises to reinforce learning through observation and practice. Focused on the AQ Ability skills, such as resilience, grit, mental flexibility, and unlearning. Let me bring this to life with an example:

A pharmaceutical company that was striving to streamline and optimize a crucial drug testing process.

Consider Dr. Anaya, the director of clinical trials, who noticed that the current testing process was taking too long and faced several bottlenecks, delaying the time to market for potentially life-sav-

ing medications. *Recognizing that a streamlined and optimized process was required, Dr. Anaya chose to apply her adaptability intelligence, specifically her mental flexibility, to find a solution.*

Recognizing the complexity of the problem, she understood that a single solution approach would be limiting and time-consuming. Instead, she decided to experiment with multiple strategies simultaneously. To do this, she divided her team into smaller groups and assigned each one to focus on a different potential solution.

One group was tasked with redefining the testing process to eliminate non-value-adding steps. Another was asked to explore innovative technologies that could automate some of the procedures. The third group focused on improving communication and coordination with external testing laboratories.

Dr. Anaya encouraged each group to operate independently, giving them the freedom to test, adapt, and learn from their experiments. The concurrent experiments enabled parallel learning experiences, effectively reducing the overall time needed for process improvement.

After several weeks, each group presented their findings. The outcome was a comprehensive set of improvements, each contributing to an overall more efficient process, from a new automated technology to a streamlined communication protocol with the labs.

By maintaining an open mindset to multiple possible solutions and fostering an environment of concurrent learning and experimentation, Dr. Anaya significantly shortened the development time for a new and improved clinical trial process. Her approach not only accelerated the timeline to launch but also built a culture of adaptability and continuous learning within her team.

Create opportunities for employees to work on cross-functional teams or projects, allowing them to observe and learn from colleagues with diverse perspectives and skill sets.

By applying the principles of Albert Bandura's Social Learning Theory, L&D professionals can create learning experiences that promote the development of AQ, ultimately preparing employees to thrive in an ever-changing work environment.

7.4.3 RECOGNIZING AND CELEBRATING LEARNING ACHIEVEMENTS

Recognizing and celebrating learning achievements play a vital role in fostering a culture of continuous development and maintaining employee motivation. Research has shown that recognition and appreciation can significantly contribute to job satisfaction, engagement, and commitment to the organization. L&D professionals can effectively implement recognition programs that acknowledge employees' accomplishments and reinforce the importance of lifelong learning.

Positive Reinforcement: According to the principles of operant conditioning, developed by B.F. Skinner, reinforcing desired behaviors with positive consequences increases the likelihood that those behaviors will be repeated. By providing praise, rewards, or other forms of recognition for learning achievements, L&D professionals can strengthen employees' commitment to their professional development.

The Progress Principle: Teresa Amabile and Steven Kramer's research on the progress principle suggests that acknowledging and celebrating small wins and incremental progress can have a significant impact on employee motivation and performance. L&D professionals can apply this concept by regularly highlighting employees' learning milestones, encouraging them to reflect on their progress, and celebrating their achievements, no matter how small they may seem.

To effectively recognize and celebrate learning achievements, consider creating a formal recognition program that acknowledges employees' learning accomplishments, such as completing a course, earning a certification, or mastering a new skill. Share success stories through company newsletters, intranet, or social media platforms to highlight employees' learning achievements and inspire others to pursue their development. Organize regular learning celebrations or events, where employees can come together to share their learning experiences, exchange insights, and celebrate their accomplishments. Encourage managers to recognize and celebrate their team members' learning achievements during team meetings, performance reviews, or one-on-one sessions.

7.5 NAVIGATING ORGANIZATIONAL CHANGE AND DISRUPTION

As experienced L&D professionals, you play a crucial role in preparing your organization for change and disruption. As you know, the world is evolving at an unprecedented pace, and organizations must adapt to stay competitive. To build mental flexibility, adaptability, and agility within your workforce, it is essential to support leaders in driving change effectively. You must design impactful strategies that enable leaders to navigate and lead change successfully.

7.6 SUPPORTING LEADERS IN DRIVING CHANGE

I n the words of Peter Drucker, *"Whenever anything is being accomplished, it is being done, I have learned, by a monomaniac with a mission."* We might also say this is true of change. Whenever something is being changed, it invariably starts with a monomaniac before it becomes a widespread movement. These monomaniacs are our leaders, the driving force behind change, and therefore equipping them with the right skills, knowledge, and tools is crucial for successful transformation. L&D professionals must focus on developing leadership courage and competencies that can help leaders inspire their teams, navigate change, and drive organizational growth.

Develop emotional intelligence: According to Daniel Goleman's influential work on emotional intelligence, leaders who demonstrate high emotional intelligence are better equipped to manage change, foster positive work environments, and lead their teams effectively. Encouraging leaders to develop self-awareness, empathy, and effective communication skills is critical to navigtae change successfully. However, you would be right in thinking that nobody wants to be told bluntly to their face "You need to develop empathy and self-awareness." Consider how these skills can be framed and packaged in a way that is appealing and "speaks the language" of the leader in question. Emotional intelligence starts with you: what are *they* hoping to get out of this experience?

Cultivate adaptability intelligence (AQ): Adaptability intelligence, as explained in Ross Thornley's book "Decoding AQ," is the ability to recognize, understand, and navigate change effectively. By fostering AQ in leaders, you can help them embrace uncertainty, develop resilience, and adjust their strategies to meet the evolving needs of the organization. Encourage leaders to assess their current adaptability levels, identify areas for improvement, and develop AQ by training their mental flexibility, resilience, and unlearning skills. This focus on AQ will better prepare leaders to guide their teams through change and disruption.

Enhance decision-making skills: Leaders must make critical decisions in times of change and disruption. Let's draw from the works of Daniel Kahneman and Amos Tversky on decision-making, teach leaders how to recognize cognitive biases and use analytical thinking to make informed choices.

Daniel Kahneman and Amos Tversky are renowned psychologists whose work has significantly contributed to our understanding of human decision-making. They identified several cognitive biases that often affect our choices and proposed ways to mitigate their impact.

Overconfidence Bias: Leaders often overestimate their

knowledge, underestimating risks and potential problems. L&D professionals should train leaders to recognize this bias and encourage them to seek diverse perspectives and adopt a mindset of intellectual humility.

Anchoring Bias: This is the tendency to rely too heavily on the first piece of information (the "anchor") when making decisions. Leaders should be encouraged to seek additional data points and challenge initial information to avoid this bias.

Confirmation Bias: People tend to favor information that confirms their preconceptions. Leaders can be trained to actively seek contradictory evidence and consider alternatives to combat this bias.

Hindsight Bias: This occurs when people believe they could have predicted an event after it has occurred. This can lead to overconfidence in future predictions. L&D professionals should help leaders understand the unpredictability of certain events and promote a learning attitude rather than a blaming culture.

Framing Effect: People often react differently to the same information depending on how it's presented or framed. Teaching leaders about this bias can help them communicate more effectively, especially in critical situations that require change. This can be very powerful when we use the insights from the AQ Character data, as to why someone adapts, to increase engagement, unlock flow and reduce friction.

By incorporating these insights from Kahneman and Tversky's work into L&D programs, professionals can help leaders make more informed and unbiased decisions. This is especially crucial in times of change and disruption, where clear, objective decision-making can significantly impact an organization's adaptability and resilience.

Build change management capabilities: Familiarize leaders with established change management models, such as Kotter's 8-Step Change Model or the ADKAR Model, to help them understand and implement effective change strategies within their organizations.

Encourage agile leadership: To navigate the fast-paced business environment, leaders must embrace agile thinking and adapt to changing circumstances quickly. Provide training on agile leadership principles and practices to help leaders create more flexible and responsive organizations.

Strengthen communication and storytelling skills: Effective communication is essential during organizational change. Leaders must be able to articulate the reasons behind change and inspire their teams to embrace it. Teach leaders ways of crafting compelling narratives that motivate employees and promote buy-in. Whilst the art of storytelling is not easily attained (hence why writers spend decades honing their craft), there are tried and trusted techniques for bringing your story home that can be learned by anyone.

Collaborate with cross-functional teams: Encourage leaders to engage with cross-functional teams and external partners to gain diverse perspectives and insights on change initiatives. This collaboration can result in more innovative and effective solutions to the challenges faced during periods of disruption.

Developing these critical competencies in your organization's leaders will better prepare your workforce for change and disruption, ensuring continued growth and success.

As a highly experienced L&D professional, your role extends beyond delivering effective learning programs. You are instrumental in fostering a culture of continuous learning, supporting organizational change, and preparing your workforce for the future. By embracing advanced strategies and staying ahead of industry trends, you can maximize the impact of your L&D initiatives and drive lasting success for your organization.

CHAPTER 8: DEVELOPING ADAPTIVE LEADERSHIP

In today's volatile, uncertain, complex, and ambiguous (VUCA) world, organizations need leaders who are agile, adaptable, and equipped with the skills necessary to navigate the constantly changing landscape. In this chapter we will delve into the concept of adaptive leadership, its key components, and how to support the growth and development of leaders who possess this crucial skill set.

Adaptive leadership goes beyond traditional leadership approaches by emphasizing the ability to learn, adapt, and excel in situations characterized by uncertainty and rapid change. We will explore the essence of adaptive leadership, the role of adaptability intelligence (AQ), decision-making in uncertain times, and fostering innovation and creativity. We will also discuss how to create a supportive culture for leadership growth, and measure the impact of adaptive leadership development programs. By understanding and implementing these principles, you can help cultivate the next generation of leaders who are prepared to navigate the challenges of the modern world.

8.1 THE ESSENCE OF ADAPTIVE LEADERSHIP

A daptive leadership is a critical skill for today's leaders, who must navigate an increasingly complex and dynamic business environment. In the past 25 years, I, have observed firsthand how the ability to adapt and learn in the face of change has become more crucial than ever before. Adaptive leaders possess a unique combination of skills and mindsets that enable them to thrive in the face of uncertainty, change, and ambiguity. They are able to pivot quickly, embrace new ideas, and respond effectively to emerging challenges.

As we transition from the 'knowledge economy' to the 'imagination economy,' a leader's *'speed of learning'* is essential for adaptive leadership in an exponential world. Leaders must develop their ability to learn rapidly to stay ahead of the curve and maintain their competitive edge. By understanding and developing the core elements of adaptability intelligence (AQ), effective decision-making in uncertain times, and fostering innovation and creativity, leaders can build resilience, cultivate mental flexibility, and create a culture of continuous learning and improvement in their organizations.

8.1.1 ADAPTABILITY INTELLIGENCE (AQ)

S tart your organization's adaptability journey by discovering your team's who, why and when—i.e.

who is most likely to change, why they change, and what environments facilitate (or even catalyst) change. The best way to do this is by implementing the AQme science-backed assessment at *aqai.io*

8.1.2 DECISION-MAKING IN UNCERTAIN TIMES

Adaptive leaders must be adept at making decisions in uncertain and ambiguous situations. The ability to think critically, trust one's intuition, and utilize data effectively is paramount for the leaders of today to navigate the complex landscape and make well-informed choices that benefit their organizations. However, the challenge lies in the fact that, in uncertain times, relevant data might not yet exist, requiring leaders to embrace rapid experimentation, real-time feedback loops, increased bravery, and gut-instinct in their decision-making process.

Critical thinking involves the ability to evaluate information objectively, identify underlying assumptions, and consider multiple perspectives before reaching a conclusion. When data is scarce or incomplete, adaptive leaders must now learn to instigate rapid experimentation and feedback loops to test their hypotheses and gather insights. This could take the form of problem-solving exercises, scenario planning, and simulations that challenge leaders to think deeply about the issues at hand and weigh the potential outcomes of various courses of action, while also encouraging them to learn from each iteration.

Intuition will play a more significant role in deci-sion-mak-ing, particularly when data is scarce or incomplete. Whilst in the west, we are circumspect of intuition, viewing it as perhaps a "nebulous" and unscientific concept, there is a growing body of research into the stark reality of the "gut in-stinct" or "gut intelligence". Whilst there is not sufficient scope to go into this in detail in this book, in broad terms adaptive leaders draw from their wealth of experience, using their intu-ition to identify patterns and make connections that might not be immediately apparent. The bravery to trust your instincts and make decisions based on intuition can be the difference between stagnation and innovation. We must help leaders de-velop their intuition—and courage—by encourag-ing self-re-flection, facilitating discussions of past experienc-es, and pro-viding opportunities for leaders to learn from their mistakes (and their successes too).

In an era of abundant information, data-driven deci-sion-making is still essential, but leaders must be prepared to face situations where data is not yet available. In these cases, they need to embrace an experimental mindset, which involves taking more so called 'risks', learning from the outcomes, and iterating on their decisions.

The most adaptable and successful teams are those who transition from a structure and process focused on 'mitigating and managing risk' to one that embraces, leans into, and takes multiple risks. This shift begins with low-stakes situations, where teams can develop the necessary muscles and processes to change their perception of risk. By doing so, these teams can move away from relying solely on past known solutions and proactively unlearn those that no longer serve as accelerants for growth. Instead, they can adopt new methodologies, behaviors, and processes that facilitate innovation and adaptability.

Facilitate this change by designing programs that develop risk-taking competencies and promote a growth mindset. By providing safe spaces for teams to experiment, fail, and learn from their mistakes, organizations can help employees shift their perspective on risk and see it as an opportunity for growth rather than a threat to be avoided. Having insight – such as data gleaned from an AQme assessment – into which employees may struggle more with this mindset shift is invaluable.

As teams develop the ability to embrace risk and learn from their experiences, they become more agile and adaptable, better equipped to navigate the challenges of a rapidly changing business landscape. In turn, this newfound adaptability empowers teams to seek out and implement novel approaches, fostering a future-oriented mindset that drives innovation, resilience, and long-term success.

One way to begin building this competency in your leadership teams is to use **The Futures Wheel methodology**.

8.1.3 THE FUTURES WHEEL

A visual brainstorming technique developed by Jerome C. Glenn in the 1970s, **The Futures Wheel** is designed to help individuals and organizations explore the potential consequences of a specific decision, trend, or event in a structured and systematic way. The methodology aims to identify direct and indirect consequences, revealing the possible future implications and impacts that may arise from the initial change. By using the Futures Wheel, decision-makers can gain a better understanding of the complex relationships between various factors and make more informed decisions based on the potential outcomes.

Here's a step-by-step guide to using the Futures Wheel methodology:

Define the central issue or event: Begin by identifying the central issue, trend, or event that you want to analyze. Write it down in the center of a large sheet of paper or on a whiteboard.

Identify first-order consequences: Consider the immediate or direct consequences that might result from the central issue. Write these consequences around the central issue, connecting them with lines to indicate that they are direct outcomes.

Identify second-order consequences: For each of the first-order consequences, think about the indirect or secondary consequences that could result from them. Write these down and connect them to the first-order consequences with lines.

Identify further-order consequences: Continue this process of identifying consequences for each new layer, moving outward from the central issue. You can go as deep as necessary to explore the full range of potential impacts.

Analyze the Futures Wheel: Review the completed Futures Wheel and look for patterns, interconnections, and potential opportunities or challenges that emerge. Consider the implications of each consequence on your organization or decision-making process.

Develop strategies and action plans: Based on your

analysis of the **Futures Wheel**, develop strategies or action plans to address the identified consequences. This may involve capitalizing on potential opportunities, mitigating risks, or adapting to the anticipated changes.

The **Futures Wheel** exercise not only helps organizations anticipate potential consequences, but it also contributes to building **mental flexibility**, a critical component of Adaptability Intelligence (AQ). Mental Flexibility is the ability to observe the current, to see things for what they are, together with the ability to create new pathways, to change them with effective action, if indeed you deem it necessary to do so. Dr Michael Sinclar defines psychological flexibility as, *"The ability to contact your present moment experience, without defence, as fully as possible as a conscious human being. To change or persist in behaviour so you can move towards the stuff you really care about in life; what you value. To be mindfully aware of thoughts and feelings and to commit to value-based living".*

This enables more effective decision-making and problem-solving. By engaging in the **Futures Wheel** exercise, individuals and teams practice considering multiple perspectives, outcomes, and potential scenarios. This process fosters mental agility and an openness to new ideas.

Furthermore, when the **Futures Wheel** exercise is conducted with cross-departmental collaborations, it facilitates the exchange of diverse insights and perspectives from various functional areas within the organization. This diversity enriches the ideation process and encourages the consideration of a broader range of potential consequences and opportunities.

To take this one step further, regularly use the **Futures Wheel Methodology** to systematically explore the possible rami-fications of their decisions or trends and develop more com-prehensive strategies that account for the complexities and uncertainties of the future.

8.1.4 FOSTERING INNOVATION AND CREATIVITY

Innovation and creativity allow leaders to devise new strategies and uncover unique solutions to complex problems. Here are a few ideas to support the development of innovation and creativity in leaders:

Provide a diverse learning environment: As we mentioned in chapter 1.3, new ideas can be very threatening to individuals working at every level of the organisation, including leaders. Therefore, obtaining buy-in is critical before trying to introduce leaders to new methodologies or "influence" them. However, once that buy-in is obtained, there should be a relationship of trust that will allow you to implement new systems and approaches. For example, creating a diverse learning environment to promote learning opportunities from a wider range of field and disciplines.

Encourage structured ideation sessions: Facilitate structured ideation sessions that promote the free flow of ideas while setting clear objectives and guidelines. This approach helps leaders generate more ideas and encourages them to challenge conventional wisdom, and embrace unconventional perspectives while maintaining focus on the ultimate goal.

Teach leaders to embrace ambiguity: Equip leaders with the skills to navigate uncertain situations and make decisions with incomplete information. This can be achieved by offering training in **scenario planning, futures thinking, and probabilistic reasoning**, which can help leaders better understand and manage uncertainty.

Foster a culture of psychological safety: We have mentioned this before, but it is worth iterating again. Create an environment where leaders feel comfortable taking risks, sharing ideas, and admitting mistakes. Encourage open communication, provide constructive feedback, and celebrate both successes and learning experiences.

Promote experiential learning: Encourage leaders to learn through experimentation and hands-on experiences, such as simulations or real-world projects. This approach can help leaders develop the ability to think creatively and adapt to changing circumstances.

8.1.5 SCENARIO PLANNING

Scenario planning is a strategic method that helps leaders anticipate and prepare for various potential futures. It involves creating and analyzing multiple plausible scenarios to understand the implications of different choices and trends. By engaging in scenario planning, leaders can better navigate uncertainty and make informed decisions.

→ IDENTIFYING KEY TRENDS AND UNCERTAINTIES

→ DEVELOPING A RANGE OF PLAUSIBLE SCENARIOS

→ ANALYZING THE POTENTIAL IMPACT OF EACH SCENARIO

→ IDENTIFYING COMMON THEMES AND STRATEGIC RESPONSES

→ CONTINUOUSLY UPDATING SCENARIOS AS NEW INFORMATION BECOMES AVAILABLE

Here is a simple how-to guide for developing scenario planning:

> → GATHER A DIVERSE GROUP OF INDIVIDUALS TO BRING MULTIPLE PERSPECTIVES.
>
> → IDENTIFY CRITICAL UNCERTAINTIES AND DRIVING FORCES THAT COULD IMPACT YOUR ORGANIZATION OR INDUSTRY.
>
> → CREATE A RANGE OF PLAUSIBLE SCENARIOS BASED ON THESE UNCERTAINTIES AND FORCES.
>
> → ANALYZE THE POTENTIAL CONSEQUENCES, CHALLENGES, AND OPPORTUNITIES PRESENTED BY EACH SCENARIO.
>
> → DEVELOP STRATEGIC RESPONSES AND CONTINGENCY PLANS BASED ON YOUR FINDINGS, AND REGULARLY UPDATE YOUR SCENARIOS AS NEW INFORMATION EMERGES.

8.1.6 FUTURES THINKING

Futures thinking is a mindset and approach that encourages leaders to consider the long-term implications of their decisions. It involves exploring different possibilities, anticipating change, and understanding the potential impact of various trends and developments on the organization's future.

→ EMBRACING A LONG-TERM PERSPECTIVE

→ IDENTIFYING EMERGING TRENDS AND POTENTIAL
DISRUPTIONS

→ CONSIDERING MULTIPLE POSSIBLE FUTURES

→ DEVELOPING FORESIGHT AND ANTICIPATION SKILLS

→ CONTINUOUSLY MONITORING AND UPDATING YOUR
UNDERSTANDING OF THE FUTURE LANDSCAPE

A simple how-to guide for developing futures thinking:

→ CONDUCT RESEARCH AND STAY INFORMED ABOUT
EMERGING TRENDS, TECHNOLOGIES, AND POTENTIAL
DISRUPTIONS.

→ ENGAGE IN REGULAR BRAINSTORMING SESSIONS
WITH DIVERSE STAKEHOLDERS TO EXPLORE VARIOUS
FUTURE POSSIBILITIES.

→ DEVELOP THE HABIT OF CONSIDERING LONG-TERM
CONSEQUENCES WHEN MAKING DECISIONS.

→ USE TOOLS SUCH AS THE FUTURES WHEEL TO
MAP POTENTIAL IMPACTS AND IMPLICATIONS OF
DECISIONS.

→ CONTINUOUSLY MONITOR THE EVOLVING LANDSCAPE
AND ADJUST YOUR UNDERSTANDING AND

STRATEGIES ACCORDINGLY.

8.1.7 PROBABILISTIC REASONING

Probabilistic reasoning is a decision-making skill that involves assessing the likelihood of various outcomes and making informed decisions based on those probabilities. It helps leaders make better choices in uncertain situations by considering the range of possible results and their associated risks.

→ QUANTIFYING UNCERTAINTY AND ASSESSING PROBABILITIES

→ ANALYZING RISK AND POTENTIAL REWARDS

→ INCORPORATING STATISTICAL THINKING INTO DECISION-MAKING

→ LEVERAGING DATA AND EVIDENCE TO INFORM CHOICES

→ CONTINUOUSLY UPDATING PROBABILITIES AS NEW INFORMATION BECOMES AVAILABLE

A simple how-to guide for developing probabilistic reasoning:

→ DEVELOP A FOUNDATIONAL UNDERSTANDING OF

PROBABILITY AND STATISTICS.

→ WHEN MAKING DECISIONS, IDENTIFY THE RANGE OF POSSIBLE OUTCOMES AND ASSIGN PROBABILITIES TO EACH.

→ WEIGH THE POTENTIAL RISKS AND REWARDS OF EACH OPTION, CONSIDERING THEIR ASSOCIATED PROBABILITIES.

→ USE DATA AND EVIDENCE TO INFORM YOUR ASSESSMENTS AND CONTINUOUSLY UPDATE YOUR PROBABILITIES AS NEW INFORMATION EMERGES.

→ PRACTICE PROBABILISTIC THINKING BY REGULARLY ENGAGING IN EXERCISES SUCH AS FORECASTING AND ESTIMATION.

8.2 SUPPORTING THE DEVELOPMENT OF ADAPTIVE LEADERS

Every organization needs to cultivate leaders within its own ranks. This is advantageous for a number of reasons. In the military, it's well known that whilst officers, such as captains, may technically be of higher rank than a sergeant, the sergeant is deferred to in key situations because they have spent more time on the battlefield, more time with their particular squad (and therefore know the people, know the capabilities, and know the dynamics), and have the necessary experience to tackle emergent problems. We must also remember that a leader is not just one person at the very top of a pyramid. On the contrary, to continue the example of the military, all kinds of leaders are needed in every detachment (or department) of the organization. The general may oversee the entire army, but the general cannot control the army without sergeants, lieutenants, and corporals. Similarly, organisations need managers, directors, executives, and team leaders—across all their faculties. These leaders will need to possess the ability to navigate ambiguity, embrace uncertainty, and lead their organizations through continuous transformation. Your role in fostering adaptive leadership is crucial, and this section will guide you through the process of supporting and nurturing these invaluable leaders.

A new perspective on leadership which I personally align more with is discribed well in the book *"Leading Without Authority"* by Keith Ferrazzi with a refreshing and modern perspective on leadership, challenging traditional, hierarchical notions of authority. The main ideas in the book revolve around co-elevation, networked teams, and leading through influence rather than positional power.

Co-Elevation: Ferrazzi introduces the concept of co-elevation, a reciprocal commitment to each other's success, as the foundation for his new model of leadership. In co-elevation, all team members are committed to achieving common goals, and each individual is invested in the success of others.

Networked Teams: Ferrazzi posits that organizations should transition from traditional hierarchical structures to networked teams. In a networked team, all members are empowered to take initiative and make decisions. Everyone is encouraged to lead and contribute regardless of their formal position within the organization. This model is more flexible and adaptable, essential for thriving in today's fast-paced, dynamic business environments.

Leading through Influence: The book emphasizes that the essence of leadership today is influence, not authority. It encourages leaders to cultivate relationships, demonstrate empathy, and build trust to inspire and motivate others. This form of leadership can be more effective in engendering collaboration and driving results. You might ask - How do I lead through influence? - Here are some key actions you can take:

→ BUILD RELATIONSHIPS WITH THE RIGHT PEOPLE. PUT YOUR INTERPERSONAL SKILLS TO USE.

→ ADAPT TO OTHER PEOPLE'S WORK STYLES. EVERYONE WORKS DIFFERENTLY.

→ BE A TEAM PLAYER.

→ **HELP WHEN YOU CAN.**

→   **SIMPLIFY THINGS FOR PEOPLE.**

→   **ARTICULATE YOUR VALUE.**

→   **SPREAD POSITIVITY.**

Generosity and Authenticity: Ferrazzi encourages leaders to show generosity and authenticity, fostering deeper connections and relationships with their teams. He believes that by showing vulnerability and sharing personal stories, leaders can create stronger bonds, which are vital in a co-elevating work environment.

Growth and Learning: Finally, Ferrazzi underscores the importance of continuous learning and growth for leaders. By embracing a mindset of curiosity and openness to new experiences, leaders can adapt to change, overcome challenges, and lead their teams towards success.

The journey of developing adaptive leaders starts with identifying potential candidates who possess the essential traits and mindsets, designing comprehensive leadership development programs tailored to their unique needs, and creating a supportive organizational culture that encourages growth. Empowering current and future leaders to adapt, innovate, and drive success for their organizations in an increasingly

THE FUTURE-READY L&D PROFESSIONAL

complex and unpredictable landscape.

8.2.1 ASSESSING AND IDENTIFYING POTENTIAL LEADERS

Identifying individuals with the potential to become adaptive leaders and nurturing them requires a keen understanding of the key traits, behaviors, and mindsets that embody adaptive leadership. Assessment tools like AQai's AQme can aid in this process. The most valuable future leaders will be ones who can shift from 'knowing the answers' to embracing 'experimentation and imagination', providing a safe place for their teams to learn in-line with daily work, as it shifts and adapts at an exponential rate.

Assessment tools can be of great help in the identification process, offering insights into an individual's strengths, weaknesses, and growth potential. Most highly successful coaches advocate not for using one tool as the be-all and end-all oracle, but rather combining tools to produce unique insights and develop a more holistic picture. Some popular tools include per-sonality assessments, 360-degree feedback, and situational judgment tests. Additionally, observing employees in various situations, such as cross-functional projects, team collaborations, and challenging tasks, can provide valuable information about their potential to thrive as adaptive leaders.

Korn Ferry Leadership Architect: This competency-based assessment tool helps organizations identify leadership potential by measuring individuals against a comprehensive framework of leadership traits and skills. The Leadership Architect is designed to evaluate a person's abilities in critical areas such as strategic thinking, decision-making, and emotional intelligence. The assessment results can be used to create customized development plans, guide succession planning, and support talent management initiatives.

AQai's AQme Assessment: AQme is a science-backed evaluation tool designed to measure an individual's Adaptability Quotient (AQ). AQ is the ability to effectively navigate change and uncertainty. The AQme assessment helps individuals, teams, and organizations understand their adaptability strengths and areas for improvement, providing insights that can be leveraged for personal and professional growth.

Upon completing the assessment, participants receive a personalized report with detailed insights into their adaptability strengths and areas for development. The report also includes tailored recommendations and actionable steps to help individuals enhance their AQ, ultimately improving their ability to cope with change and uncertainty.

Organizations can use AQai's AQme assessment to identify high-potential employees, inform targeted development programs, and foster a culture of adaptability and resilience. By understanding and cultivating adaptability, organizations can better navigate the complexities of the modern world and drive lasting success.

Once potential leaders have been identified, it's essential to provide them with opportunities to develop and hone their skills. This can include assigning them to challenging projects, providing them with coaching and mentoring, and encouraging them to take on new responsibilities.

8.2.2 CREATING A SUPPORTIVE CULTURE FOR LEADERSHIP GROWTH

Creating a supportive organizational culture that promotes the development of adaptive leaders is essential for fostering a resilient and agile workforce. The following engaging strategies will empower potential leaders and drive their growth, while offering an alternative perspective on leadership development:

Embrace Reverse Mentoring: Implement a reverse mentoring program where younger or less experienced employees mentor more experienced colleagues. This encourages open-mindedness, adaptability, and fosters a culture where everyone is seen as a valuable source of knowledge and insight.

Implement Stretch Assignments: Encourage potential leaders to take on projects or tasks that are outside their comfort zone or current skill set. This helps them develop resilience, problem-solving skills, and adaptability as they navigate new challenges and learn from their experiences.

Organize Cross-disciplinary Workshops: Facilitate workshops that bring together employees from various departments and backgrounds to collaborate on problem-solving and idea generation. This exposes potential leaders to different perspectives and ways of thinking, helping them develop the adaptability needed for effective leadership.

Practice Deliberate Reflection: Encourage leaders to engage in deliberate reflection exercises, a practice supported by research as a powerful tool for developing self-awareness and adaptability. Schedule regular "reflection breaks" or implement reflection journals where leaders can document their thoughts, experiences, and learnings. By intentionally analyzing their actions, decisions, and the outcomes they produce, leaders can identify areas for growth and develop more adaptive behaviors and mindsets.

Conduct Future-Back Workshops: Host workshops that encourage leaders to envision their organization's future success and work backward to identify the steps, skills, and mindsets required to achieve it. This approach, backed by research in strategic foresight and scenario planning, helps leaders to develop long-term thinking, foster adaptability, and better anticipate and prepare for change. By embracing a future-back perspective, leaders can better understand the potential challenges and opportunities that lie ahead, allowing them to navigate uncertainty with greater confidence and agility.

Introduce Cognitive Reappraisal Techniques: Teach leaders cognitive reappraisal techniques, which have been supported by research in cognitive psychology as a way to manage emotions and foster resilience. These techniques involve reinterpreting and reframing situations or events to change one's emotional response. By practicing cognitive reappraisal, leaders can better handle stress, uncertainty, and setbacks, ultimately enhancing their adaptability and mental flexibility.

Create Microlearning Opportunities: Implement microlearning modules that focus on specific skills or topics related to adaptability and mental flexibility. Doing these in-flow with daily work can help deepen the learning culture. It is widly known that breaking down complex subjects into smaller, more manageable learning units can increase retention and engagement. By offering frequent, easily digestible learning opportunities, you can support continuous development and encourage leaders to embrace change and adapt more readily.

8.3 MEASURING THE IMPACT OF ADAPTIVE LEADERSHIP DEVELOPMENT

The realms of adaptability, EQ, intuition, and wisdom are not as easily quantified as those of finance or marketing, hence why "measuring" the success of these initiatives can seem daunting or even impossible. This section will guide you through the process of defining success metrics, tracking progress, and making data-driven adjustments to your approach. Furthermore, it will provide insights on demonstrating the return on investment (ROI) of your adaptive leadership development programs, ensuring that you can communicate their value to stakeholders and secure ongoing support for your initiatives.

8.3.1 DEFINING SUCCESS METRICS

Identifying the appropriate success metrics for your development initiatives is vital to evaluate the effectiveness of your efforts. Utilizing relevant frameworks can streamline the process of determining which outcomes to measure, such as increased adaptability, improved decision-making, and enhanced innovation within your organization.

8.3.2 TRACKING PROGRESS AND ADJUSTING YOUR APPROACH

Regularly assess the effectiveness of your leadership development programs and make data-driven adjustments as needed. Learn how to use feedback, analytics, and performance metrics to continually refine your approach and ensure maximum impact. See chapter 7.2 for a range of evaluation methods explained.

8.3.3 DEMONSTRATING THE ROI OF ADAPTIVE LEADERSHIP DEVELOPMENT

Showcase the value of your development efforts by quantifying their impact on organizational performance. Discover different ROI methodologies you can use for your programs to engage stakeholders and secure ongoing support for your initiatives.

Developing adaptive leadership is essential for organizations seeking to thrive in today's rapidly changing landscape. By understanding the key skills and mindsets of adaptive leaders, you can design and deliver effective development programs that empower leaders to adapt, innovate, and drive lasting success for organizations.

CHAPTER 9: MEASURING THE IMPACT OF L&D INITIATIVES

9.1 UNDERSTANDING THE IMPORTANCE OF EVALUATION

Evaluation is a critical aspect of L&D, as it allows professionals to assess the effectiveness and impact of their initiatives. Explore the reasons why measuring the impact of L&D is essential and how it contributes to the continuous improvement of your practice.

9.2 EVALUATION METHODS AND MODELS

There are various evaluation methods and models that you can use to assess the impact of your initiatives. Let's dive into some of the most widely used models, such as Kirkpatrick's Four Levels of Evaluation, Phillips ROI Methodology, The Balance Scorecard, OKR's, Impact Mapping, and Brinkerhoff's Success Case Method.

9.2.1 KIRKPATRICK'S FOUR LEVELS OF EVALUATION

Kirkpatrick's Four Levels of Evaluation is a widely recognized and respected model for evaluating the effectiveness of training programs. Developed by Dr. Donald Kirkpatrick in the late 1950s, this model provides a framework to measure the success of a training program by assessing four distinct levels: Reaction, Learning, Behavior, and Results. The model is grounded in the understanding that each level of evaluation builds upon the previous one, ultimately leading to a comprehensive understanding of the training's impact.

The first level, Reaction, assesses the participants' satisfaction with the training program. This level focuses on the trainees' immediate perceptions, typically gathered through surveys or questionnaires. The second level, Learning, measures the extent to which the participants have acquired the intended knowledge, skills, and attitudes as a result of the training. Pre- and post-training assessments or testing can be used to gauge the learning that has occurred. The third level, Behavior, examines the degree to which participants apply what they have learned in their day-to-day work. This level can be assessed through observation, feedback from supervisors, or self-assessment. Finally, the fourth level, Results, evaluates the tangible outcomes of the training program, such as increased productivity, improved quality, or reduced costs. This level often requires more time and resources to measure, as the outcomes may not be immediately apparent.

Key aspects of the Kirkpatrick's Four Levels of Evaluation include:

→ A HIERARCHICAL STRUCTURE: EACH LEVEL BUILDS ON THE PREVIOUS ONE, ENSURING A COMPREHENSIVE EVALUATION OF THE TRAINING PROGRAM.

→ VERSATILITY: THE MODEL CAN BE APPLIED TO VARIOUS TYPES OF TRAINING PROGRAMS AND INDUSTRIES, MAKING IT WIDELY APPLICABLE.

→ FOCUS ON BOTH QUALITATIVE AND QUANTITATIVE DATA: THE MODEL INCORPORATES BOTH TYPES OF DATA, PROVIDING A WELL-ROUNDED UNDERSTANDING OF THE TRAINING'S IMPACT.

→ EMPHASIS ON CONTINUOUS IMPROVEMENT: BY IDENTIFYING AREAS OF SUCCESS AND AREAS THAT NEED IMPROVEMENT, ORGANIZATIONS CAN REFINE THEIR TRAINING PROGRAMS OVER TIME.

→ STAKEHOLDER ENGAGEMENT: THE MODEL ENCOURAGES INPUT FROM MULTIPLE STAKEHOLDERS, SUCH AS PARTICIPANTS, TRAINERS, AND SUPERVISORS, ENSURING A COMPREHENSIVE EVALUATION.

9.2.2 PHILLIPS ROI METHODOLOGY

Phillips ROI Methodology is a comprehensive evaluation framework developed by Dr. Jack J. Phillips. This method goes beyond Kirkpatrick's Four Levels of Evaluation by adding a fifth level: Return on Investment (ROI). The Phillips ROI Methodology assesses the financial impact of a training program, allowing organizations to determine if the benefits of the training outweigh the costs.

The first four levels of the Phillips ROI Methodology are similar to Kirkpatrick's model, evaluating Reaction, Learning, Behavior, and Results. The fifth level, ROI, is calculated by comparing the monetary benefits of the training program, such as increased productivity or reduced errors, to the costs of implementing the program. The ROI is expressed as a percentage, providing a clear indicator of the training program's financial value. This methodology helps organizations prioritize and allocate resources to training programs that demonstrate the highest potential for a positive return on investment.

Key aspects of Phillips ROI Methodology include:

→ **COMPREHENSIVE EVALUATION:** THE METHOD ASSESSES THE TRAINING PROGRAM'S EFFECTIVENESS AT MULTIPLE LEVELS, INCLUDING ITS FINANCIAL IMPACT.

→ **RETURN ON INVESTMENT (ROI):** THE FIFTH

LEVEL OF EVALUATION ALLOWS ORGANIZATIONS TO
DETERMINE THE FINANCIAL VALUE OF THE TRAINING
PROGRAM.

→ *FOCUS ON BOTH QUALITATIVE AND
QUANTITATIVE DATA:* THE METHODOLOGY
COMBINES DIFFERENT TYPES OF DATA TO PROVIDE A
WELL-ROUNDED UNDERSTANDING OF THE TRAINING'S
IMPACT.

→ *DECISION-MAKING TOOL:* THE ROI CALCULATION
CAN BE USED TO PRIORITIZE AND ALLOCATE
RESOURCES FOR TRAINING PROGRAMS THAT
DEMONSTRATE THE HIGHEST POTENTIAL FOR
POSITIVE FINANCIAL OUTCOMES.

→ *BENCHMARKING:* BY MEASURING ROI,
ORGANIZATIONS CAN COMPARE THE EFFECTIVENESS
OF DIFFERENT TRAINING PROGRAMS OR BENCHMARK
THEIR PROGRAMS AGAINST INDUSTRY STANDARDS.

9.2.3 OKRS (OBJECTIVES AND KEY RESULTS)

OKRs (Objectives and Key Results) is a goal-setting framework championed by companies such as Google, LinkedIn, and Twitter. It was introduced by Andy Grove, the former CEO of Intel, and later popularized by John Doerr, a venture capitalist who introduced the concept to Google in its early days.

How OKRs work: An Objective (O) is a clear, concise statement of a goal to be achieved. It's qualitative and provides direction on where to go. Key Results (KR) are the specific, measurable actions required to achieve the objective. They are quantitative and define how success will be measured. Typically, an Objective will have 2-5 Key Results.

For example, an objective for an L&D team might be "Improve employee engagement in learning programs". Corresponding Key Results could be "Increase course completion rates to 80%" and "Achieve an average course feedback score of 4.5/5".

Value of OKRs: The power of OKRs comes from their simplicity, focus, and alignment. They encourage teams to focus on the most important goals, thus reducing wasted effort. OKRs also promote alignment across different levels of the organization, as each individual, team, and department's OKRs should support the company's overall objectives.

Companies using OKRs and their results: Google is perhaps the most famous example of a company that has embraced OKRs. The approach helped Google maintain focus and alignment as it grew from a small startup to a global tech giant.

LinkedIn and Twitter have also reported improved clarity and alignment as a result of implementing OKRs. More recently, smaller tech companies and even non-tech organizations have begun to adopt OKRs due to their simplicity and effectiveness.

Advantages: OKRs offer a number of benefits, including improved focus on key goals, better alignment across the organization, increased transparency, and a culture of learning and continuous improvement. By making goals visible and measurable, OKRs create a shared understanding of what success looks like and how to achieve it.

Implementing OKRs requires commitment from all levels of the organization, as well as a culture that supports transparency, collaboration, and continuous learning. Despite the challenges, many organizations have found that the benefits of OKRs far outweigh the effort required to implement them.

> → *OBJECTIVES ARE QUALITATIVE, INSPIRATIONAL, AND TIME-BOUND STATEMENTS OF WHAT AN ORGANIZATION AIMS TO ACHIEVE.*
>
> → *KEY RESULTS ARE QUANTITATIVE, MEASURABLE INDICATORS THAT DEMONSTRATE PROGRESS TOWARDS THE OBJECTIVE.*
>
> → *OKRS PROMOTE TRANSPARENCY AND ACCOUNTABILITY, AS THEY ARE TYPICALLY SHARED*

> → ACROSS THE ORGANIZATION.
>
> → OKRS ARE REVISITED REGULARLY (USUALLY QUARTERLY) TO TRACK PROGRESS AND MAKE NECESSARY ADJUSTMENTS.

The framework fosters a culture of continuous learning, as it encourages organizations to set ambitious goals and learn from both successes and failures.

9.2.4 THE BALANCED SCORECARD

A strategic management framework that helps organizations to monitor and manage their performance across multiple dimensions. It focuses on four primary areas: financial, customer, internal processes, and learning and growth.

> → THE FINANCIAL PERSPECTIVE ASSESSES PROFITABILITY, REVENUE GROWTH, AND COST MANAGEMENT.
>
> → THE CUSTOMER PERSPECTIVE EVALUATES CUSTOMER SATISFACTION, RETENTION, AND MARKET SHARE.
>
> → THE INTERNAL PROCESSES PERSPECTIVE EXAMINES EFFICIENCY, QUALITY, AND INNOVATION IN OPERATIONS.

> → THE LEARNING AND GROWTH PERSPECTIVE LOOKS AT EMPLOYEE DEVELOPMENT, ORGANIZATIONAL CULTURE, AND THE CAPACITY FOR CHANGE.

By aligning goals and measures across these perspectives, the Balanced Scorecard helps organizations to achieve a well-rounded approach to performance management.

9.2.5 THE IMPACT MAPPING TECHNIQUE

A visualization tool that helps organizations to identify the relationships between desired outcomes, behaviors, and interventions. It provides a clear understanding of how different elements contribute to the achievement of specific goals.

> → THE TECHNIQUE STARTS BY DEFINING THE DESIRED OUTCOMES OR GOALS OF AN INITIATIVE.
>
> → NEXT, IT IDENTIFIES THE KEY BEHAVIORS OR ACTIONS THAT ARE NECESSARY TO ACHIEVE THOSE OUTCOMES.
>
> → THE THIRD STEP INVOLVES DETERMINING THE INTERVENTIONS OR STRATEGIES THAT WILL ENCOURAGE AND SUPPORT THE DESIRED BEHAVIORS.
>
> → BY CONNECTING THE OUTCOMES, BEHAVIORS, AND INTERVENTIONS, AN IMPACT MAP IS CREATED, WHICH

> SERVES AS A VISUAL REPRESENTATION OF THE
> RELATIONSHIPS BETWEEN THESE ELEMENTS.

The Impact Mapping Technique helps organizations to identify the most effective interventions, monitor progress, and measure the impact of their initiatives.

9.2.3 BRINKERHOFF'S SUCCESS CASE METHOD

Brinkerhoff's Success Case Method (SCM) is a practical, results-oriented evaluation approach developed by Dr. Robert Brinkerhoff. It focuses on identifying the most and least successful instances of a training program's implementation to understand what factors contribute to success or failure. This method combines both qualitative and quantitative data to provide rich insights into the effectiveness of a training program and identify areas for improvement.

The SCM starts by defining clear objectives for the training program and identifying the expected outcomes. Then, evaluators gather data from the most successful and least successful participants through interviews, surveys, or other methods. By analyzing these success cases, organizations can pinpoint the factors that contribute to success, such as support from supervisors or the application of specific skills. Conversely, analyzing the least successful cases helps identify barriers to success or areas that require additional attention. The findings from the SCM can be used to refine and improve the training program, ensuring better outcomes and a higher return on investment.

Key aspects of Brinkerhoff's Success Case Method include:

→ **FOCUS ON SUCCESS AND FAILURE CASES:** ANALYZING THE BEST AND WORST INSTANCES PROVIDES VALUABLE INSIGHTS INTO THE FACTORS THAT INFLUENCE THE TRAINING PROGRAM'S EFFECTIVENESS.

→ **QUALITATIVE AND QUANTITATIVE DATA:** THE METHOD COMBINES BOTH TYPES OF DATA, OFFERING A COMPREHENSIVE UNDERSTANDING OF THE TRAINING'S IMPACT.

→ **ADAPTABILITY:** THE SCM CAN BE APPLIED TO A WIDE RANGE OF TRAINING PROGRAMS AND INDUSTRIES.

→ **IMPROVEMENT-ORIENTED:** THE INSIGHTS GAINED FROM THE METHOD ARE USED TO REFINE AND IMPROVE THE TRAINING PROGRAM.

→ **REAL-WORLD APPLICATION:** THE SCM FOCUSES ON EVALUATING HOW THE TRAINING IS APPLIED IN THE PARTICIPANTS' WORK CONTEXT, PROVIDING

ACTIONABLE INSIGHTS FOR IMPROVEMENT.

9.3 KEY METRICS FOR MEASURING L&D IMPACT

In order to effectively evaluate the impact of your L&D initiatives, it is essential to identify the most important metrics that align with your organization's goals and objectives. By tracking and analyzing these key performance indicators (KPIs), you can make data-driven decisions that optimize your learning programs and demonstrate their value to stakeholders. This section will delve into the following critical metrics for measuring L&D impact:

Learner Satisfaction: This metric evaluates the overall experience of participants in your learning programs. It is crucial to assess learner satisfaction to ensure that the content and delivery methods are engaging, relevant, and useful. You can gather feedback through surveys, focus groups, or interviews.

Knowledge Retention: The ultimate goal of any L&D initiative is to ensure that participants retain and apply the knowledge they have acquired. Assessing knowledge retention can be done through pre- and post-assessments, quizzes, or practical exercises that test the learners' understanding and recall of the material.

Behavior Change: To measure the effectiveness of your L&D programs, it is essential to evaluate whether participants have implemented new skills and behaviors in their day-to-day work. You can assess behavior change by conducting follow-up assessments, observing workplace performance, or gathering feedback from managers and peers.

Business Results: The impact of L&D initiatives should ultimately be visible in the organization's performance. Linking learning programs to specific business outcomes, such as increased productivity, improved customer satisfaction, or reduced employee turnover, can help demonstrate their value. You can track these outcomes through performance metrics, key performance indicators (KPIs), or other business-related data.

Return on Investment (ROI): Calculating the ROI of your L&D initiatives involves comparing the financial benefits of the program (e.g., increased revenue or cost savings) to the costs of implementation and maintenance. Demonstrating a positive ROI can help secure ongoing support and investment in your learning programs.

9.4 IDENTIFYING AREAS FOR IMPROVEMENT

For experienced L&D professionals, identifying areas of improvement in your initiatives requires a more sophisticated approach. One key aspect to focus on is leveraging advanced data analytics and artificial intelligence (AI) to optimize the content of your learning programs. By analyzing patterns in learner engagement, performance, and feedback, you can identify specific content areas that may require enhancements, such as incorporating new research, addressing knowledge gaps, or incorporating diverse perspectives. Staying informed on the latest industry trends and best practices will ensure your programs remain relevant and effective.

Based on the insights gained from evaluation data, experienced L&D professionals should be proactive in adjusting their strategies to better meet the needs of learners and the organization. This may involve reallocating resources, redesigning programs, or rethinking your overall approach to L&D. As you adapt your strategy, consider incorporating emerging technologies, exploring alternative learning methods, and fostering a culture of continuous improvement that encourages experimentation and innovation.

Effectively communicating the impact of your L&D initiatives to stakeholders, such as executives and managers, is a critical skill for experienced L&D professionals. Using the data collected through evaluation methods, showcase the return on investment (ROI) of your programs and demonstrate how they contribute to the achievement of organizational goals. By presenting a compelling narrative backed by data, you can secure ongoing support for your initiatives and position yourself as a strategic partner within the organization.

Measuring the impact of L&D initiatives is crucial for ensuring their effectiveness and continuously improving your L&D practice. By utilizing a variety of evaluation methods (shared in 7.2) and metrics, L&D professionals can make data-driven decisions that optimize their initiatives and demonstrate their value to stakeholders. With a relentless focus on improvement, adaptability, and innovation, you can transform your L&D practice and help your organization thrive in the age of rapid change.

CHAPTER 10: BUILDING A FUTURE-READY L&D COMMUNITY

10.1 THE VALUE OF COLLABORATION AND NETWORKING IN L&D

Collaboration and networking are essential for L&D professionals who aim to stay current with industry trends and best practices. Discover the benefits of connecting with your peers, sharing experiences, and learning from one another to build a future-ready L&D community.

For more experienced L&D professionals, collaboration and networking involves not only staying current with in-dus-try trends and best practices but also engaging in thought lead-ership and contributing to the development of innovative L&D strategies. By connecting with your peers, you can co-create solutions to complex challenges in the field.

One of the best ways L&D professionals can broaden their network is through leveraging technology, connecting with global experts and thought leaders. Online platforms, webi-nars, and virtual conferences provide invaluable opportunities to exchange ideas, discuss challenges, and develop new approaches to learning and de-velopment.

10.2 ESTABLISHING PARTNERSHIPS

Forming partnerships with other L&D professionals, organizations, and experts can provide valuable resources and support for your L&D initiatives. Explore strategies for identifying potential partners, establishing mutually beneficial relationships, and leveraging partnerships to enhance your L&D practice. For the more experienced L&D professional, forming partnerships should go beyond traditional collaborations to include strategic alliances that drive transformational change in the L&D landscape. In addition to enhancing your practice, these partnerships can lead to the co-creation of novel learning solutions, research collaborations, and advocacy for policies and standards that promote excellence in L&D.

Building partnerships within your organization can help you better align L&D initiatives with organizational goals and objectives. It is essential to collaborate with key stakeholders, such as HR, IT, and senior management, to create a unified approach to L&D. Embedding a learning culture throughout the organization and fostering cross-functional collaboration

External partnerships, such as those with industry experts, technology providers, and other L&D professionals, can offer fresh perspectives and resources. Discover how to identify and engage with external partners to enhance your L&D practice.

10.3 SHARING KNOWLEDGE AND BEST PRACTICES

Sharing knowledge and best practices among L&D professionals is crucial for the continued growth and development of the L&D community. By sharing your experiences, lessons learned, and successes with others you can contribute to the collective wisdom of the profession. Let's banish "knowledge hoarding" as it is a hindrance to growth and shift to actively promote and practice "knowledge sharing," recognizing that in the expansion of collective wisdom, we enrich our own capabilities and contribute meaningfully to the broader L&D community.

Engage in L&D-focused professional forums, groups, and online communities to exchange ideas, discuss challenges, and share best practices with your peers. Learn how these collaborative spaces can help you stay informed about the latest trends and developments in L&D.

Participate in industry conferences, workshops, and events to network with other L&D professionals, learn about cutting-edge research and innovations, and contribute to the ongoing conversation surrounding L&D.

By contributing to the collective wisdom of the profession, you can foster an environment that values continuous improvement and innovation. Let's explore some practical examples and a step-by-step guide to help you share your experiences, lessons learned, and successes with others.

Step 1: Identify the knowledge or best practices you want to share

Begin by reflecting on your L&D experiences and identifying specific insights, techniques, or strategies that have been particularly effective in your practice. Consider which elements of your work could be valuable to other professionals and which lessons learned could help others avoid pitfalls or improve their own practice.

Step 2: Choose the right format and platform

There are various formats and platforms available for sharing knowledge, such as blog posts, case studies, webinars, and podcasts. Consider which format is best suited for communicating your insights and which platform is most likely to reach your intended audience. For example, if you have a detailed case study to share, writing a blog post or creating a presentation for a conference might be the most effective approach.

Step 3: Create engaging and informative content

When crafting your content, focus on making it engaging, informative, and actionable. Provide clear examples and evidence to support your claims, and offer practical advice that others can apply to their own L&D practice. Make sure to provide context by explaining the background of your experience and highlighting the challenges and opportunities you encountered along the way.

Step 4: Share your content with the L&D community

Once your content is ready, share it with the L&D community through relevant channels. This could include posting it on your own website or blog, submitting it to industry publications or forums, or presenting it at conferences and events. You can also leverage social media platforms like LinkedIn to share your content with a broader audience.

Step 5: Engage with your audience and gather feedback

After sharing your content, engage with your audience by responding to comments, questions, and feedback. Encourage open dialogue and discussion, and be open to constructive criticism. This will help you refine your ideas, improve your content, and further contribute to the L&D community.

5 Practical Examples:

Write a **case study** on a successful L&D initiative you implemented, detailing the challenges faced, strategies employed, and the impact on the organization. Share this case study on your blog or submit it to industry publications.

Organize a **webinar** or workshop to share a specific best practice or technique that has proven effective in your L&D practice. Invite other L&D professionals to attend and exchange their own experiences and insights.

Create a **podcast** series featuring interviews with other L&D professionals, exploring their successes, challenges, and best practices in the field. Share these episodes on social media platforms and L&D forums to foster dialogue and knowledge sharing.

Launch a virtual "**L&D Book Club**" where L&D professionals come together to read and discuss relevant books or articles in the field. This initiative can foster collaboration and knowledge sharing, allowing participants to exchange ideas, explore new perspectives, and discover innovative approaches. Utilize video conferencing tools and online discussion boards to facilitate these discussions, making them accessible to a wide audience.

Host a series of "**L&D Lightning Talks,**" where L&D professionals present brief, impactful presentations on a specific topic, lesson learned, or best practice from their experience. These short, focused talks can be delivered in person or via an online platform, allowing for efficient knowledge sharing. Invite diverse speakers from different industries, backgrounds, and areas of expertise to create a rich and varied learning experience for participants.

By following these steps and sharing your knowledge and best practices, you can contribute to the growth and development of the L&D community and help create a future-ready profession.

Embrace the experiences and successes of other L&D professionals as opportunities for learning and growth. Understand how to integrate valuable insights from your peers into your own L&D practice to stay ahead in the ever-evolving L&D landscape.

Actively seek feedback from colleagues, partners, and learners to continuously improve your L&D initiatives. Use this feedback to refine your practice, identify new opportunities for growth, and adapt to the changing needs of your organization and industry.

Fostering a future-ready L&D community requires ongoing collaboration, networking, and learning from others. By establishing partnerships, sharing knowledge, and building on the successes of your peers, you can stay ahead and ensure the continued growth and success of your L&D practice.

CHAPTER 11 : EMBRACING THE FUTURE OF L&D

11.1 HARNESSING NEUROPLASTICITY: PIONEERING BRAIN-COMPATIBLE L&D STRATEGIES FOR THE FUTURE

Understanding the brain's capacity to change - its neuroplasticity - is pivotal for enhancing our approach to learning and development. How can we apply this knowledge to foster environments that synergize with our inherent learning processes? I believe the potential is immense.

Learning and re-skilling, from a neuroscientific perspective, are associated with changes at multiple levels of brain structure and function, including neuroelectrical, neuroanatomical, neurophysiological, and neurochemical. It's important to note that while our understanding of these processes is growing, there is still much that is not fully understood.

Neuroelectrical: Learning, particularly the formation of memories, is associated with changes in the electrical activity of the brain. For instance, patterns of neuronal firing, known as oscillatory rhythms or "brain waves," can become synchronized during learning tasks, facilitating communication between different brain regions.

Neuroanatomical: Learning and re-skilling lead to changes in brain anatomy at both the macro and micro scales. Macroscopically, learning can increase the volume of certain brain areas. For instance, the hippocampus, which is critical for memory, can expand in size following intensive learning tasks. Microscopically, learning is associated with synaptic plasticity, the ability of the connections between neurons (synapses) to change in strength and number. The phrase "neurons that fire together wire together" captures the principle that repeated and persistent activation of a particular neural pathway strengthens the synaptic connections along that pathway, making future activation more likely – a phenomenon known as long-term potentiation (LTP).

Neurophysiological: Neurophysiology deals with the functioning of the nervous system. At this level, learning involves changes in the excitability and firing rates of neurons. For instance, through the process of LTP, the same input will produce a larger output, indicating that the synapse has become more efficient at transmitting signals.

Neurochemical: Learning and re-skilling also involve a host of neurochemical changes, primarily related to neurotransmitters and neuromodulators. For example, the neurotransmitter glutamate plays a crucial role in LTP. Furthermore, the release of dopamine, a neurotransmitter often associated with reward, can signal the value of a particular outcome, thereby promoting learning based on reward prediction. Serotonin, another neurotransmitter, is also thought to modulate learning processes, although its specific role is less well understood.

These changes all contribute to the brain's remarkable plasticity – its ability to reorganize itself by forming new neural connections throughout life. This plasticity underpins our capacity to learn new skills, adapt to change, and recover from brain injury. As the field of neuroscience progresses, our understanding of these processes will continue to deepen, promising exciting advances in learning and education.

The science of neuroplasticity and learning can provide invaluable insights for the development programs we create. Here are a few ways you can think about it.

Emphasize Active Learning: Active learning promotes the changes in synaptic strength that underpin long-term memory. Encourage strategies such as practice, quizzing, teaching others, and real-world application of skills.

Encourage Regular Breaks: Learning is consolidated during rest periods, not during the actual training. This relates to the way neurochemicals function during the learning process. Scheduling regular breaks during training sessions can help facilitate this consolidation.

Design for Rewarding Learning Experiences: Dopamine, associated with reward, has a crucial role in learning. If you can design training programs that are rewarding and engaging, you are more likely to get better results. This could include gamification of learning or providing immediate positive feedback.

Promote Social Learning: The social aspect of learning engages different regions of the brain and promotes the formation of strong memories. You can leverage this by encouraging group work, collaborative problem-solving, and learning from peers.

Support Lifelong Learning: Neuroplasticity, the brain's ability to change and adapt, happens throughout life. It's essential to create a culture that supports continuous learning and skill development.

Mindfulness and Stress Management: Chronic stress can negatively impact neuroplasticity and learning. Implementing mindfulness and stress management training can help enhance your employees' learning capacity.

Consider Multimodal Learning: Different types of information (visual, auditory, etc.) are processed in different regions of the brain, so using a range of teaching methods can help engage more of the brain and promote better learning.

Remember, everyone's brain is unique, and people have different learning preferences. The key is to create a diverse and flexible L&D program that can cater to the needs of all your employees.

Envision L&D programs tailored to the individual neurophysiology of our team members. By appreciating the role of neurochemicals in learning, we could design training that maximizes dopamine release for enhanced motivation and retention. By understanding the neuroanatomical basis of learning, we could formulate strategies that exploit the brain's natural preference for multimodal learning. And appreciating the neuroelectrical aspect of learning could open doors to innovative, personalized feedback mechanisms in real-time.

Looking ahead, I see a future where our grasp of neuroscience helps us create L&D initiatives that respect and leverage our brain's innate learning processes. This is a more humane, more effective, and indeed a more thrilling prospect for the future of learning and development. As stewards of this future, we are not just shaping better workers but cultivating better human beings who can adapt and thrive in our ever-evolving world. We have a magnificent opportunity - let's seize it.

As we reach the end of this book, it is important to reflect on the journey we have taken together to become future-ready L&D professionals. Throughout, we have explored various aspects of learning and development, from understanding the rapidly changing landscape to adopting new tools and strategies. The central theme of this journey has been the importance of adaptability, growth, and technology in shaping the future of learning and development.

In rapidly transforming world, the L&D profession must be ready to adapt and thrive in the face of constant change. This requires a commitment to continuous learning, a growth mindset, and the ability to embrace new technologies and methodologies. By staying agile and open to change, L&D professionals can ensure that their organizations remain competitive and relevant in today's fast-paced, knowledge-driven economy.

11.2 UNLEASHING IMAGINATION: THE NEXT PHASE OF THE EMPLOYEE LIFE-CYCLE

As we transition from a knowledge-based economy to an imagination-based one, our perspective on employee development needs to evolve. The traditional focus on knowledge retention should give way to a broader emphasis on fostering and retaining the power of imagination. In our modern world, where knowledge is becoming vastly more accessible through technology and artificial intelligence, the true differentiator lies in our ability to imagine, innovate, and solve the complex problems of tomorrow.

In the past, the value of an employee was often measured by the breadth and depth of their knowledge and experience.

The more information they had at their fingertips, the more valuable they were perceived to be. This model worked well for a time, now with the advent of technology and AI has drastically changed the landscape. With knowledge now just a voice command away, the value of simply knowing something has diminished. We live in a world where anyone can now build a complex app in a day, with simple prompts in natural language, iterate and deploy a functioning tool. It is pervasive and will transform every industry within the next 2 to 3 years. What's crucial now is not just what we know but what we can imagine and do with that knowledge. How quickly we can unlearn, and relearn.

This shift to an imagination economy places a premium on creativity, innovation, rapid experimentation and adaptability skills. It's no longer enough to merely process and regurgitate information; employees must now be able to interpret, extrapolate, and create from the information they have. They must be able to imagine new ideas, devise innovative solutions, and foresee the implications of their decisions.

In this new paradigm, L&D professionals are tasked with nurturing the imaginations of their employees. This means encouraging curiosity, promoting creative thinking, and creating a culture where original ideas are celebrated. It also involves providing opportunities for employees to exercise their imaginations, such as through cross-departmental sprints, innovation challenges, and cross-functional projects.

Moreover, it's not just about fostering imagination in the first place – it's also about retaining it. Over time, it's easy for routine and complacency to stifle creativity. L&D professionals must actively work against this by continually providing fresh stimuli, challenging assumptions, and promoting a growth mindset. They should encourage employees to step outside their comfort zones, learn from other industries and disciplines, and approach problems from new angles.

A high AQ indicates a readiness to embrace change, learn new skills, and adapt to new technologies – all of which are crucial in the imagination economy.

As we move into the imagination economy, it's vital that we shift our focus from retaining knowledge to unleashing imagination. This will require rethinking our approach to L&D, but with the right mindset and tools, we can nurture the creativity and adaptability that will drive our future success.

As L&D professionals, our role is not only to facilitate learning for others but also to be lifelong learners ourselves. This means staying informed about the latest trends, research, and best practices, as well as regularly reflecting on our own practice to identify areas for improvement. By cultivating a spirit of curiosity and a willingness to learn from our experiences and those of our peers, we can continue to grow and develop as professionals.

Technology will continue to play a significant role in the future of L&D, as new tools and platforms emerge to support more effective and engaging learning experiences. As L&D professionals, it is essential to stay abreast of these technological advancements and be prepared to integrate them into our practice when appropriate. By harnessing the power of technology, we can create more personalized, interactive, and impactful learning experiences for our learners.

Ultimately, the future of L&D lies in our ability to embrace change and adapt to the evolving needs of our learners, organizations, and the world at large. By remaining adaptable, committed to growth, and open to technological innovation, we can ensure that our L&D practice remains future-ready and capable of driving meaningful, lasting change.

In closing, let us remember that the journey to becoming a future-ready L&D professional is not a destination but an ongoing process. As the landscape of learning and development continues to shift and evolve, we must be prepared to adapt, learn, and grow alongside it. By embracing the future of L&D with enthusiasm, curiosity, and resilience, we can help shape a brighter, more adaptive, and more successful future for ourselves, our organizations, and the learners we serve.

BONUS: 12 PRACTICAL WAYS L&D PROFESSIONALS CAN USE GPT-4 IN YOUR DAILY WORK

In this bonus chapter, we explore ten practical ways learning and development (L&D) professionals can harness the power of GPT-4 to enhance their daily work and improve their organization's learning culture.

→ **CONTENT CREATION:** USE GPT-4 TO GENERATE EDUCATIONAL MATERIALS, SUCH AS ARTICLES, CASE STUDIES, AND TRAINING MANUALS. WHILST IT'S NOT QUITE SO SIMPLE AS PRESSING A BUTTON AND HAVING A FULLY POLISHED ARTICLE, GPT-4 CAN HELP WITH THE INITIAL DRAFT WORK AND IDEATION, WHICH AS ANY WRITER WILL TELL YOU IS ONE OF THE TOUGHEST ASPECTS OF CREATION. THIS CAN SAVE TIME AND EFFORT, ALLOWING L&D PROFESSIONALS TO FOCUS ON OTHER ASPECTS OF THEIR WORK.

→ **TRAINING NEEDS ANALYSIS:** UTILIZE GPT-4 TO ANALYZE EMPLOYEE PERFORMANCE DATA AND IDENTIFY SKILL GAPS, HELPING TO PINPOINT THE MOST RELEVANT AND VALUABLE TRAINING OPPORTUNITIES FOR YOUR ORGANIZATION.

→ **COURSE DESIGN:** GPT-4 CAN HELP IN DESIGNING

COMPREHENSIVE TRAINING MODULES AND COURSES, INCORPORATING BEST PRACTICES AND THE LATEST INDUSTRY TRENDS TO ENSURE THE TRAINING IS RELEVANT AND ENGAGING.

→ **PERSONALIZED LEARNING:** LEVERAGE GPT-4 TO CREATE TAILORED LEARNING PATHS AND RESOURCES FOR INDIVIDUAL EMPLOYEES, TAKING INTO ACCOUNT THEIR UNIQUE LEARNING STYLES, INTERESTS, AND SKILL LEVELS.

→ **INTERACTIVE LEARNING ACTIVITIES:** USE GPT-4 TO DEVELOP INTERACTIVE LEARNING ACTIVITIES, SUCH AS QUIZZES, SIMULATIONS, AND GAMES, WHICH CAN HELP MAKE THE LEARNING EXPERIENCE MORE ENGAGING AND ENJOYABLE.

→ **COACHING AND MENTORING:** GPT-4 CAN BE USED TO GENERATE PERSONALIZED COACHING SUGGESTIONS, TIPS, AND INSIGHTS FOR EMPLOYEES, ENHANCING THE EFFECTIVENESS OF ONE-ON-ONE COACHING AND MENTORING SESSIONS.

→ **EMPLOYEE ONBOARDING:** STREAMLINE THE ONBOARDING PROCESS BY UTILIZING GPT-4 TO GENERATE CUSTOMIZED WELCOME MATERIALS, GUIDELINES, AND RESOURCES THAT ADDRESS THE SPECIFIC NEEDS AND REQUIREMENTS OF NEW HIRES.

→ **KNOWLEDGE MANAGEMENT:** GPT-4 CAN BE EMPLOYED TO DEVELOP AN INTELLIGENT

KNOWLEDGE MANAGEMENT SYSTEM THAT CAN SEARCH, ANALYZE, AND SUMMARIZE INFORMATION FROM VARIOUS SOURCES, MAKING IT EASIER FOR L&D PROFESSIONALS TO ACCESS AND SHARE KNOWLEDGE WITHIN THE ORGANIZATION.

→ **EVALUATION AND FEEDBACK:** USE GPT-4 TO ANALYZE EMPLOYEE FEEDBACK AND TRAINING EVALUATIONS, IDENTIFYING TRENDS, AREAS FOR IMPROVEMENT, AND SUCCESS STORIES THAT CAN INFORM FUTURE L&D INITIATIVES.

→ **COLLABORATION AND NETWORKING:** GPT-4 CAN FACILITATE COLLABORATION AMONG L&D PROFESSIONALS BY GENERATING IDEAS, DISCUSSION PROMPTS, AND PROBLEM-SOLVING SUGGESTIONS, FOSTERING A CULTURE OF CONTINUOUS LEARNING AND DEVELOPMENT.

By incorporating GPT-4 into their daily work, L&D professionals can optimize their efforts, create more engaging and effective learning experiences, and ultimately drive organizational growth and success.

STEP-BY-STEP BEGINNERS GUIDE AND PROMPT RECOMMENDATIONS/EXAMPLES FOR EACH PRACTICAL WAY TO USE GPT-4:

Initially you can 'steer' how you want the responses from ChatGPT-4, to respond in a way most useful and helpful. For example before each of the following examples you could start with something like this:

"You are and L&D professional with 25 years experience. You write relatable, concise and readable text without stop words, filler words or Jargon. Your personality tone is neutral between professional and casual, slightly more relaxed than serious, encouraging, optimistic and positive, with short snappy sentences. Draw inspiration from the best L&D publications, science and peer reviewed papers."

Then add your request. It also helps to share examples you have, and be specific in how you want the response to output. Such as use bullet points, or respond in a table format. A great tip is to also input "**ask questions before responding**" this will help ensure your response is as helpful to you as possible.

CONTENT CREATION:

a. Identify the topic and learning objectives.

b. Input a prompt that outlines the desired content, for example:

"Create a comprehensive article on project management best practices, including sections on planning, communication, and risk management."

c. Review and edit the generated content to ensure

---

accuracy and relevance.

TRAINING NEEDS ANALYSIS:

a. Gather employee performance data and key skill requirements.

b. Input a prompt asking GPT-4 to analyze the data and identify skill gaps, for example:

"Analyze the provided employee performance data to determine the most significant skill gaps and recommend relevant training opportunities."

c. Use the generated insights to inform your training strategy.

COURSE DESIGN:

a. Determine the course topic, objectives, and target audience.

b. Input a prompt for GPT-4 to design a course outline, for example:

"Design a comprehensive training course on effective communication for remote teams, including modules on virtual meetings, asynchronous communication, and building rapport."

c. Refine the generated course outline and develop the necessary course materials.

PERSONALIZED LEARNING:

a. Collect information about individual employees' learning preferences, skill levels, and interests.

b. Input a prompt for GPT-4 to create tailored learning paths, for example:

"Create a personalized learning plan for Employee A, focused on improving their leadership skills and taking into account their preference for hands-on learning activities."

c. Monitor employee progress and adjust the learning paths as needed.

INTERACTIVE LEARNING ACTIVITIES:

a. Identify the learning objectives and desired level of interactivity.

b. Input a prompt for GPT-4 to generate activity ideas, for example:

"Generate three engaging and interactive learning activities to teach conflict resolution skills in a team setting."

c. Develop the activities based on the generated ideas and incorporate them into your training programs.

COACHING AND MENTORING:

a. Collect information about the employee's goals,

challenges, and progress.

b. Input a prompt for GPT-4 to generate coaching suggestions, for example:

"Provide coaching tips and insights for Employee B to help them overcome challenges related to time management and prioritize their workload effectively."

c. Use the generated suggestions to guide your coaching and mentoring sessions.

EMPLOYEE ONBOARDING:

a. Determine the specific needs and requirements of new hires.

b. Input a prompt for GPT-4 to create customized onboarding materials, for example:

"Generate a tailored onboarding guide for a new software engineer, including an introduction to the company culture, an overview of the development processes, and resources for further learning."

c. Review and distribute the generated materials to new hires.

KNOWLEDGE MANAGEMENT:

a. Identify the key sources of information and knowledge within your organization.

b. Input a prompt for GPT-4 to develop a knowledge management system, for example:

"Create an intelligent knowledge management system that can search, analyze, and summarize information from various sources, such as internal documents, industry reports, and expert articles."

c. Implement the generated system and train employees on how to use it effectively.

EVALUATION AND FEEDBACK:

a. Collect employee feedback and training evaluation data.

b. Input a prompt for GPT-4 to analyze the data, for example:

"Analyze the provided employee feedback and training evaluations to identify trends, areas for improvement, and success stories that can inform future L&D initiatives."

c. Use the generated insights to adjust and improve your L&D programs.

COLLABORATION AND NETWORKING:

a. Identify the key stakeholders and areas for collaboration within the L&D community.

b. Input a prompt for GPT-4 to generate ideas for

fostering collaboration and networking, for example:

"Suggest five creative strategies for fostering collaboration and networking among L&D professionals, focusing on sharing best practices, innovations, and challenges within the industry."

c. Implement the generated ideas and encourage active participation from L&D professionals in your network.

KEY STAKEHOLDER BENEFITS:

The Power of Adaptability in Today's Workplace. adaptability has emerged as a critical competency for individuals and organizations alike. With rapid technological advancements, evolving market conditions, and shifting workforce demographics, the ability to adapt and thrive in the face of change has become more important than ever. This section aims to demonstrate the key benefits of fostering adaptability for various stakeholders within an organization, from L&D professionals to CEOs and Directors of Innovation.

By enhancing adaptability within the workforce, organizations can unlock a multitude of benefits that contribute to their overall success and growth. These benefits are not limited to one area or function, but rather extend across the organization, touching every stakeholder involved. In the following pages, we will explore the specific advantages of building adaptability for L&D professionals, CFOs, CHROs, CEOs, and Directors of Innovation. By understanding and communicating the value of adaptability for each stakeholder, we can better appreciate the importance of nurturing this crucial skill in today's workplace.

As you read through the ideas, consider how you can apply these insights to your own organization and improve buy-in. Reflect on the ways in which you can contribute to building a more adaptable and resilient workforce, ready to face the challenges and opportunities of the ever-evolving business landscape.

Benefits for L&D Professionals:

a. Enhanced ability to design and deliver effective learning programs that cater to the evolving needs of the workforce.

b. Improved understanding of how to foster adaptability within teams and organizations, leading to better outcomes in training and development initiatives.

c. Increased professional value by staying ahead of industry trends and becoming a leader in the field of adaptability and learning.

Benefits for the CFO:

a. Improved financial performance through increased employee productivity and efficiency.

b. Reduced costs associated with turnover and recruitment as employees become more adaptable and resilient to change.

c. Better resource allocation as L&D initiatives become more targeted and focused on building adaptability within the organization.

Benefits for the CHRO:

a. Enhanced talent management strategies by incorporating adaptability as a key competency for employee development and growth.

b. Improved employee engagement and satisfaction, as adaptable employees are more likely to embrace change and thrive in new situations.

c. Streamlined organizational change management processes, as employees with high AQ are better equipped to handle transitions and adapt to new ways of working.

Benefits for the CEO:

a. Increased organizational agility and resilience, enabling the company to stay competitive in a rapidly changing business environment.

b. Strengthened company culture that values adaptability, continuous learning, and innovation.

c. Improved decision-making, as leaders with high AQ are

better at anticipating and responding to market shifts and disruptions.

Benefits for the Director of Innovation:

a. Enhanced innovation capabilities by fostering an adaptable workforce that is open to new ideas and can quickly adapt to change.

b. More effective collaboration and cross-functional teamwork, as employees with high AQ are more skilled at adjusting to new situations and working with diverse teams.

c. Accelerated ideation and prototyping processes, as adaptable employees are more likely to experiment, learn from failure, and iterate quickly.

ACT NOW

The journey of a thousand miles begins with a single step. Development and training at work is a complex and important topic, one that will continue to be relevant so long as human beings exist. Likewise, AQ is no ordinary subject of study, we are committed to unlocking the skills, mindsets, and environments to ensure everyone can thrive, a world where everyone can have complete future confidence no matter the context, and that no one is left behind. This book is an all-too-brief glimpse into the science and principles of AQ and how they correlate with developing people to be future-ready. In reality, each sub-dimension of AQ is a life's work to understand and improve. Angela Duckworth's book entitled *Grit* is a testament to that fact! This means it can be daunting to know where to start.

The temptation, having done an AQme assessment, is to dive immediately into our weakest sub-dimension (for example, perhaps we have low Resilience) and then frantically begin trying to improve it. However, this is reactionary.

I personally recommend starting with understanding the situation and overall goal, or desired outcomes. These are the lenses through which we can then bring meaning using the three master dimensions: AQ-Ability, AQ-Character, and AQ-Environment. If we understand how these "three inputs" interrelate, and serve the specific situational objectives, then we can leverage the best results for ourselves, our teams and for our organisations.

It is my firm belief that in harnessing AQ, we can unlock our greatest potential, as individuals and as a species.

THE PATH FORWARD - LEVERAGE AI TO EMPOWER YOUR LEADERSHIP DEVELOPMENT PROGRAMS - BOOK ON OUR WORKSHOP SERIES

As we conclude this journey, it's time to take your newfound knowledge and perspectives and transform them into action. My objective in writing this book was to not only enlighten you about the transformative power of artificial intelligence, but to inspire you to embrace it strategically and practically within your daily operations and leadership roles.

If there's one thing we've learned from our exploration, it's that the future belongs to those who adapt and innovate. Change is the only constant, and our ability to navigate this dynamic landscape hinges on our readiness to continuously learn, adapt, and innovate. And where better to start than with **'Leading in the AI Era: Leveraging GPT-4 and the Science of Adaptability to Transform Team Performance'**?

This workshop goes beyond simple knowledge acquisition - it's about understanding and implementing AI tools such as GPT-4 to streamline your work processes, enhance team efficiency, and create a lasting impact. You and your team will learn not just how to harness the potential of AI, but how to blend it seamlessly into your operations and organizational culture. This is your chance to become a leader who not only understands the future, but shapes it.

Moreover, we delve deep into the science of adaptability - your key to surviving and thriving in a rapidly evolving business landscape. You'll gain practical techniques to build resilience, foster innovation, and steer your team confidently through the complex dynamics of the digital age.

The future is here, and it's time to seize it. Your leadership effectiveness in the AI-driven world starts here, with this workshop. Don't miss this opportunity to lead your team into a future filled with potential and growth.

Remember, this is not just about understanding the technology, but truly harnessing its power to transform your leadership and your organization.

Action Steps:

→ *SECURE YOUR SPOT IN THE 'LEADING IN THE AI ERA' WORKSHOP. EMAIL PARTNERSUCCESS@AQAI.IO*

→ *EMBRACE THE JOURNEY OF BECOMING A FUTURE-READY, AI-SAVVY LEADER.*

→ *EQUIP YOUR TEAM WITH THE TOOLS AND STRATEGIES NEEDED TO SUCCEED IN THE AI ERA.*

The future waits for no one. Step forward with purpose, determination, and a vision for what you and your team can accomplish in the AI era. Remember, you're not just preparing for the future, you're creating it. Act now, and transform your leadership potential into reality.

If, as a people leader, you answer the following 7 questions with a "hell yes!", then running an AQ pilot program will be the greatest multiplier of transformational success you can gift your teams.

---

1. **You proactively want to expand the support for the mental health and wellbeing of your workforce, recognising they need help to successfully navigate the massive changes ahead.**

2. **You see innovation not just as needed but as a critical competitive advantage that will become ever more valuable through each market change.**

3. **You recognise we are living in a VUCA* world, and invest in the learning and development of your people to provide relevant and happy futures, for both your people and your organisation. *(volatility, uncertainty, complexity, and ambiguity)**

4. **You have over 50 employees.**

---

5.   You are committed to invest in understanding and improving the adaptability of your leaders and workforce. Improving your people's resilience, mindset, and motivation. Cultivating hope, engagement, and reducing stress.

6. You are committed to co-elevation and collaboration, looking for new ways to leverage relationships for the health and growth of society at large.

7.   You see an urgent need to take action now, reimagining and engaging your organisation in creating collaborative solutions to expand your future value and vision.

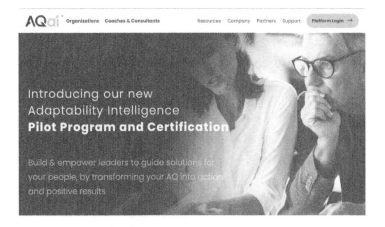

THE AQ PILOT PROGRAM

Simply put this is an **bespoke adaptability pilot program.** To help people leaders like you, to retain and develop your employees, improve wellbeing, and begin to strengthen your whole organisation's positive relationship with change.

The AQ Practitioner & Pilot Program promotes effective and engaging adaptability data, to help you identify hidden strengths and opportunities to enhance employee's abilities and skills to navigate change, at an individual, team, and organisational-wide level.

HOW DO WE DELIVER VALUE?

Having the largest and fastest growing network of adaptability-certified consultants in the world, combined with our unique people-data science, this high value program is guaranteed to deliver results.

We train, certify, and empower Talent Professionals and Leaders like you. Our hybrid learning experience involves 45 lessons, workbooks, and 4 hours of live training. Resulting in your AQ Certification with a bunch of SHRM credits too.

As we all know learning and practice is one thing, embedding and activating is another. So if you choose our AQ Pilot we shift to the practical application inside your organisation, so your newly minted knowledge doesn't gather dust in a corner of your mind, or on a shelf, but it's actually implemented with you.

So, learn by DOING, apply your new AQ skills and activate a pilot programming YOUR organisation, led by one of our Certified Adaptability Professionals and join companies such as Microsoft, Amazon, and LVMH in being some of the very first to leverage AQ solutions.

WHY NOW?

Change is happening faster than many businesses' ability to adapt.

And did you know adaptability intelligence, your AQ, is the number one most desired skill according to Linkedin Learnings annual report, and Forbes, and we believe the best predictor of life satisfaction and career success?

Employees, leaders, and companies in every corner of the world are struggling to keep pace with the changes required to stay relevant, let alone thrive. We are seeing the highest levels of workplace stress, and accelerating talent attrition.

Challenges like the great resignation, hiring freezes, massive proposition pivots, and entirely re-writing the remote and hybrid working playbook, not to mention being expected to transition to newer and newer systems and technologies constantly.

Leaders are still right in the middle of these overwhelming changes, where employees are demanding better working cultures and more flexibility; Wellbeing, performance and results are under immense pressure.

Don't let your high potential talent and most valuable leaders down. You can make a difference, right now. Not in years, or months, but within weeks.

WHAT NEXT?

Visit our website and speak to our team at AQai to learn more and even **get a made for you business case template** to help gain buy-in. *https://aqai.io/organizations/aq-pilot*

Pilot Program for Organisations

Includes certification

1. 2 week AQ Practitioner Certification

+

2. 6 week Pilot Program Launched

Includes:
- ✓ AQ Practitioner Certification course
- ✓ AQ assessments for your team
- ✓ People data and analytics, from science backed-research
- ✓ Team report and debrief
- ✓ Pilot program launched within your organisation to prove impact

45 on-demand lessons **4** hours of live training **11** SHRM credits available **4** yrs of research, science & application

Get Certified - Train & perfect your skills in AQ

Train and certify internal HR Professionals in AQ (Adaptability Intelligence) before launching a pilot program within your organisation working alongside an AQ Professional Partner. We work together to tailor the right approach and program for your needs.

A quick look in side AQ Pratitioner Certification..

100% Online	Duration	
10% One-to-One	Varies depending on your time constraints and the pace in which you wish to complete the course.	Module 1 : **Introduction**
65% Self Paced		Module 2 : **Application & Model**
25% Live Session	**typically 2-3 weeks**	Module 3 : **AQ Environment**

 Activate Pilot - We help you launch a tailored AQ Pilot program

We help you launch a pilot AQ Adaptability training program in your organization, working with a selected Certified Partner from our worldwide community. By unlocking the power of AQ you can demonstrate impact and uplift in team & business performance.

①	②	③	④	⑤
Onboard & Setup	Select & Match	Launch & Collect	Data Intelligence & Analysis	Debrief & Activate
WEEK 1	WEEK 2 & 3		WEEK 4	WEEK 5

//

For us it was obvious: if we as a company want to effectively surf the wave of constant change, we will have to strengthen our employees' adaptability and change leadership.

For us the AQme assessment is an essential part of our Accelerating Leaders' self-awareness journey that allows them to improve their adaptability and take concrete actions on their abilities.

- Nick Price, Founder

//

Join some of the most ambitious companies on the planet

ABOUT THE AUTHOR

Ross Thornley is an exponential leader, futurist, and adaptability pioneer. Living in the UK with his wife Karen, their two dogs, bee hive and rescue chickens, he balances the rapid technological world with a peaceful life in the New Forest, where they grow dozens of fruit and vegetables for their simple vegan lifestyle.

"Coach, Mentor, Entrepreneur and 'AQ' Pioneer. Author of Moonshot Innovation & AQ Decoded. Ross's work is opening up new frontiers in workplace education. Leveraging conversational AI and predictive analytics his company's platform enables people, teams and organizations to successfully navigate accelerating change. His ability to contextualize diverse and complex subjects, inspire and engage audiences makes him a highly sought after international speaker."

WALL STREET JOURNAL.

At AQai, he is co-founder, CEO and master trainer, in flow

when building the army of highly engaged and committed pioneers. Training over 250 coaches in the science and power of human adaptability in the first year of the program.

A passionate and prolific creator and educator. Amassing over 10,000 hours of workshop design, facilitation and keynotes over two decades. A serial-entrepreneur launching and growing multiple businesses across; innovation, branding, training and technology.

AQai (2018) transforming the way people and organisations adapt to change. Launching the first AQ (Adaptability Quotient) assessment and personalised digital coaching platform leveraging AI.

An eternal optimist, champion of abundance, and international speaker, he is the founder of 6 companies, including *RT Brand Communications* (2000, exit 2017), a globally trusted strategic branding agency that has worked with UN Volunteers, Thomson Reuters, Sony and numerous other blue chip clients; *Mug For Life®* (2009) a UK designed and manufactured reusable coffee cup, helping companies like HSBC, Amex, NHS, Science Museum and dozens of universities to achieve more sustainable waste policies by reduce single use disposable coffee cups and planting trees through their UK program; *Leaps®* *Innovation* (2017), a rapid, proven approach to moonshot innovation, idea generation and business challenges that empowers organisations to validate effective strategies, campaigns, new proposition development and solutions within days.

He's been a Strategic Coach® FreeZone Frontiers™ and

10X Member, Abundance A360 Member, and Singularity University Executive Program Graduate. Always excited by ambition, collaboration, and new models of thinking. Looking to connect ambitious people and solutions with communities, through creativity, intelligence and innovation.

His MTP is

TO UNITE, INSPIRE AND ACCELERATE THE BEST OF ALL HUMANITY.

www.AQai.io

https://www.linkedin.com/in/rossthornley/

OTHER BOOKS BY THE AUTHOR

MOONSHOT INNOVATION

Learn how to thrive in a world of exponential change and fulfil your highest good with a moonshot ambition.

DECODING AQ

Unlock the secrets of adaptability intelligence to harness your greatest superpower.

THE COACH'S ULTIMATE GUIDE TO LEVERAGING ADAPTABILITY

Drive client value with seven powerful principles to navigate change and leverage adaptability.

THE LEADER'S ULTIMATE GUIDE TO SUCCESSFUL TRANSFORMATION

Featuring insights from the most influencial leaders in the world: Tony Martignetti, Cameron Herold, Charlene Li, Dr. Diane hamilton, Greg Verdino, Tracy Brower, Barry O'Reilly, Dr. Benjamin Hardy, Tom Cheesewright, and John D. Anderson

Notes:

Notes:

Notes:

Notes:

Notes:

Printed in Great Britain
by Amazon